Quests and Journeys

Discovering Mythology

Quests and Journeys

Discovering Mythology

Don Nardo

Lucent Books, Inc.
P.O. Box 289011, San Diego, California

Library of Congress Cataloging-in-Publication Data

Nardo, Don, 1947–
    Quests and journeys / by Don Nardo
       p. cm.—(Discovering mythology)
Includes bibliographical references and index.
    ISBN 1-56006-855-8 (hardback : alk. paper)
    1. Voyages and travels—Mythology—Juvenile literature. [1. Voyages
and travels—Mythology. 2. Mythology.] I. Title. II. Series.
BL325.V68 N37 2002

291.1'3—dc21

                                                          2001001444

Copyright 2002 by Lucent Books, Inc.
P.O. Box 289011, San Diego, California 92198-9011

Printed in the U.S.A.

Contents

Foreword

Created by ancient cultures, the world's many and varied mythologies are humanity's attempt to make sense of otherwise inexplicable phenomena. Floods, drought, death, creation, evil, even the possession of knowledge–all have been explained in myth. The ancient Greeks, for example, observed the different seasons but did not understand why they changed. As a result, they reasoned that winter, a cold, dark time of year, was the result of a mother in mourning; the three months of winter were the days the goddess Demeter missed her daughter Persephone who had been tricked into spending part of her year in the underworld. Likewise, the people of India experienced recurring droughts, weeks and months during which their crops withered and their families starved. To explain the droughts, the Indians created the story of Vritra, a terrible demon who lived in the clouds and sucked up all the world's moisture. And the Vikings, in their search for an understanding of wisdom and knowledge, created Odin, their culture's most powerful god, who gave the world the gift of poetry and possessed two mythic ravens named Thought and Memory.

The idea of myth, fantastic stories that answer some of humanity's most enduring questions, spans time, distance, and differing cultural ideologies. Humans–whether living in the jungles of South America, along the rocky coasts of Northern Europe, or on the islands of Japan–all formulated stories in an attempt to understand their world. And although their worlds differed greatly, they sometimes found similar ways of explaining the unknown or unexplainable events of their lives. Other times, there were differences, but the method of explanation–the myth–remains the same.

Each book in the *Discovering Mythology* series revolves around a specific topic–for example, death and the underworld; monsters; or heroes–and each chapter examines a selection of myths related to that topic. This allows young readers to note both the similarities and differences across cultures and time. Almost all cultures have myths to explain creation and death, for instance, but the actual stories sometimes vary widely. The Babylonians believed that the earth was the offspring of primordial parents, while the Navajo Indians of North America assert that the world emerged over time much like an infant grows into an adult. In ancient Greek mythology, a deceased person passed quickly into the underworld, a physical place that offered neither reward nor punishment for one's deeds in life. Egyptian myths, on the other hand, contended that a person's quality of existence in the afterlife, an ambiguous state of being, depended on his actions on earth.

In other cases, the symbolic creature or hero and what it represents are the same, but the purpose of the story may be different. Although monster myths in different cultures may not always explain the same phenomenon or offer insight into the same ethical quandary, monsters nearly always represent evil. The shape-shifting beast-men of ancient Africa represented the evils of trickery and wile. These vicious animal-like creatures transformed themselves into attractive, charming humans to entrap unsuspecting locals. Persia's White Demon devoured towns-people and nobles alike; it took the intelligence and strength of an extraordinary prince to defeat the monster and save the countryside. Even the Greek Furies, although committing their evil acts in the name of justice, were ugly, violent creatures who murdered people guilty of killing others. Only the goddess Athena could tame them.

The *Discovering Mythology* series presents the myths of many cultures in a format accessible to young readers. Fully documented secondary source quotes and numerous mythological tales enliven the text. Sidebars highlight interesting stories, creatures, and traditions. Annotated bibliographies offer ideas for further research. Each book in this engaging series provides students with a wealth of information as well as launching points for further discussion.

Epic Searchers, Old and New

J ason wept as he turned his eyes away from the land of his birth. But [his men] struck the rough sea with their oars. . . . Their blades were swallowed by the waves, and on either side the dark salt water broke into foam, seething angrily in answer to the strong men's strokes. . . . All the gods looked down from heaven that day, observing *Argo* and the spirit shown by her heroic crew, the noblest seamen of their time. . . . And the wind, freshening as the day wore on, carried *Argo* on her way.[1]

These stirring words, penned by the third-century B.C. Greek poet Apollonius of Rhodes, begin one of the greatest epic quests of world mythology. In his long poem the *Argonautica*, Apollonius tells in considerable detail a tale with which everyone in his day was intimately famil- iar. This was the adventure-filled journey of the hero Jason and his crew, the Argo- nauts, to find and retrieve the fabulous Golden Fleece, the hide of a magical ram.

English novelist J. R. R. Tolkien, author of the popular Lord of the Rings *trilogy.*

Not nearly as many people today are as familiar with Jason's story. However, one would be hard-pressed to find anyone born in the past hundred years who is unfamiliar with the genre to which that story belongs. The heroic quest or journey of epic adventure has always been and remains an enduring part of human mythology, literature, films, and other entertainment media. Among the more popular recent examples are English novelist J. R. R. Tolkien's *The Lord of the Rings*, about an epic journey through an imaginary world called Middle Earth; noted film director John Ford's *The Searchers*, the story of a man's years-long attempt to track down and rescue his kidnapped niece; *Raiders of the Lost Ark*, about movie hero Indiana Jones's quest for the lost Ark of the Covenant; and *Star Trek: Voyager*, the danger-fraught trek of a crew of space explorers crossing the galaxy in search of their home.

Indeed, one is immediately struck by how much these modern examples resemble the ancient mythological ones on which they were partially based. First, the end goals of the various quests and journeys always come from a narrow list of highly coveted prizes or destinations. Wealth or some priceless or magical artifact is a common goal, for instance. Just as Indiana Jones searches for the lost ark and Jason pursues the Golden Fleece, in a famous Norse fable the god Thor tries to recover his mighty hammer. And in a classic Celtic romance, King Arthur's

The crew of the Starship Voyager. *Lost on the far side of the galaxy, they undertook a seven-year-long quest to reach earth.*

knights go looking for the Holy Grail, a cup from which Jesus Christ supposedly had drunk. Similarly, the starship *Voyager*'s journey to find home is reminiscent of the Greek hero Odysseus's ten-year voyage to reach his home after his ships are blown off course by an angry god. The other common goals of epic quests and journeys include finding the secrets of immortality (as in the ancient Mesopotamian story of the hero Gilgamesh); searching for love or lost loved ones (as in the quest of the Celtic hero Culhwch to find the fair Olwen); and attempting to find one's personal connection to nature and to God (as in the vision quests of many Native American tribes).

The characters and events of the epic quests, both old and new, are also strikingly similar. First, one or more of the searchers is invariably a hero, a larger-than-life character who proves that he can withstand the many dangers that lurk along the way. Noted modern mythologist Philip Wilkinson provides this excellent thumbnail sketch of such epic heroes:

> Strong, brave, and sometimes able to change their shape or perform other amazing feats, heroes . . . are some of the most popular characters in myth. . . . Heroes may be human or immortal; sometimes they are the offspring of a mortal and a god. Their deeds often have vital effects on human lives—heroes found tribes and cities, kill monsters, provide the necessities of life, such as fire, or teach skills such as metalworking.[2]

During their epic quests and journeys, heroes typically have to fight nature, battle monsters or other villains, and encounter gods or other spiritual forces. Jason, for example, has to deal with great rocks that threaten to crush his ship, fights fire-breathing bulls and a dragon, and is subject to the whims of quarreling goddesses. (Similarly Jason's modern counterpart, Indiana Jones, must deal with an army of snakes, battle evil Nazis, and is present when the hand of God bursts forth from the captured ark.) Without fail, the events of such quests severely test the strength, endurance, cunning, or faith of the searchers.

Why do such tales continue to fascinate us? Perhaps it is the fact that most people live ordinary lives in which they encounter few serious dangers, much less embark on journeys of epic adventure, and such fantastic, exciting stories are among the most entertaining forms of escapist fare. Or maybe deep inside each of us there is a touch of the hero, yearning to go forth and achieve admirable, seemingly impossible goals, and hearing about, reading, or watching the epic quests of ancient and modern mythology affords us a safe way to take part in such adventures. Whatever the reasons, the mythological quest is and will likely remain engrained in humanity's popular consciousness. And the tales of Jason, Odysseus, Arthur's knights, and the other epic searchers will achieve what another of their number, Gilgamesh, sought—immortality.

Gilgamesh and the Search for Immortality

Chapter One

The earliest known and still one of the greatest of all mythological quests is the Mesopotamian hero Gilgamesh's quest to find the secret of eternal life. Mesopotamia, the so-called land between the rivers, comprised the plains and hills of the great valley of the Tigris and Euphrates Rivers in what is now Iraq. This was the region in which the world's first cities rose in the late fourth millennium B.C., under an industrious, accomplished people known as the Sumerians. By the end of the third millennium B.C., Sumerian civilization had declined, and other local peoples—including the Babylonians and Assyrians—had begun to rise to prominence. Still, these peoples retained many Sumerian customs and ideas, including the Sumerian language (thereafter used mainly for sacred and literary purposes) and numerous old gods and myths.

In this way, Gilgamesh's story was preserved in the *Epic of Gilgamesh*. This is a large compilation of early heroic tales and folklore that was first collected into a unified whole around 2000 B.C. by an unknown Babylonian scribe. The story centers on the exploits of the title character, who may have been a real Sumerian ruler. According to one legend, Gilgamesh was the king of Uruk (located not far to the northwest of the Persian Gulf), which many modern scholars think may have been the world's first true city.

Whether or not Gilgamesh was a real person, the story of his fateful quest contains several elements that are larger-than-life or fantastic rather than real. The tale is, after all, a myth, a fabulous story designed not just to entertain but to explore and explain certain fundamental truths about nature and humanity. Thus,

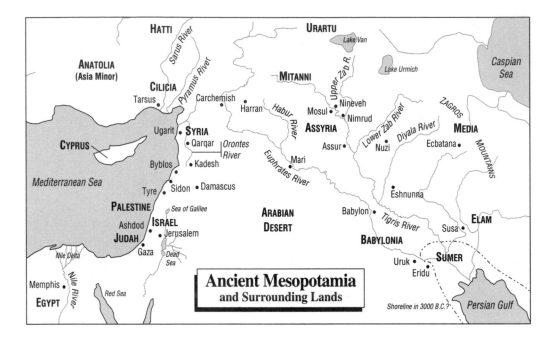

Ancient Mesopotamia
and Surrounding Lands

Shoreline in 3000 B.C.?

Gilgamesh and the other characters serve to represent or clarify larger groups, ideas, or truths. "As in Greek tragedy," says Near Eastern scholar John Gray,

> man is represented by a figure of heroic proportions, in whom the problems of human destiny may be brought into sharp focus on a spectacular stage. In the [figure of the] king, man finds his closest affinity to the gods . . . as expressed in the ancient Mesopotamian saying: "Man, being a king, who is as the image of God." Thus, the problems of mankind are reflected in the experience of King Gilgamesh, who is "two-thirds of a god and one-third human."[3]

Besides the superhuman status of the title character, other larger-than-life elements in the tale of his quest include divine intervention, several heroic feats, and an encounter with a person who had been granted the gift of immortality. That person is Utnapishtim (also called Atrahasis), a wise man and hero who saved humanity by building a large boat that enabled him and his family to survive a great flood sent by the gods. The ancient Hebrews eventually adopted his story, inserting it into the Old Testament and calling him Noah. In a story-within-the-story, Utnapishtim tells that famous tale to Gilgamesh, who wants the older man to reveal what he knows about the secret of immortality. Although Utnapishtim provides the searcher with that information, Gilgamesh is sorely disappointed by what he finds at the end of the quest.

A Goddess Intervenes in Earthly Affairs

To understand how that epic quest on behalf of humanity began, one must go back to the days when Gilgamesh first became king of the mighty city of Uruk. At first, far from being a legendary hero, Gilgamesh was a decidedly unpopular ruler. Though he was a tremendously strong, skilled, and valiant warrior whom no other man dared to challenge to a fight, he had a weakness. His weakness was that no single woman could satisfy him. Showing no tact, sensitivity, or respect for the feelings of his people, he would snatch up young girls off the streets or from the fields and force them to make love to him. This naturally raised the ire of the girls' families. However, no one dared to denounce the king for fear that he might punish or even kill them.

Finally, when they could no longer stand Gilgamesh's outrages, the city's elders went to the temple of the great mother goddess Aruru, who was Uruk's patron deity. There, they laid face-down before the goddess, who lounged serenely on her magnificent golden couch. They begged her to create a rival for Gilgamesh, someone who could match his great

In this ancient Babylonian bas-relief, Gilgamesh, hero of the first known epic quest in world literature, chases a winged demon.

strength and fighting skill. Let that rival challenge Gilgamesh and teach him a lesson, they said, so that their city might live in peace and security.

Aruru heard this plea and took pity on the beleaguered people of Uruk. As the elders watched in awe, she rose in all her shining majesty from her golden couch, strode outside, and exited the city gates. Eventually, having left the city and the sight of its residents far behind, she arrived at the riverbank. A surviving Babylonian account says that she,

washed her hands, pinched off a piece of clay, and cast it out into open country. [From the clay] she created a primitive man, Enkidu the warrior. . . . His whole body was shaggy with hair, he was furnished with tresses like a woman, his locks of hair grew luxuriant like grain. He knew neither people nor country; he was dressed as cattle are [i.e., without clothes]. With gazelles, he eats vegetation [growing in the fields], with cat-

The Historical Gilgamesh

Gilgamesh, the hero of the Mesopotamian quest for immortality, may have been a real person. The possibility of a historical Gilgamesh, as well as the historical reality of his city, Uruk, is explored here by scholar Stephanie Dalley, in *Myths from Mesopotamia*.

We know now for certain that Gilgamesh was considered in antiquity [ancient times] to be a historical character. . . . There are two different traditions concerning the parentage of Gilgamesh. The epic itself says that one Lugalbanda was his father, a man who is known. . . to have occupied the throne of Uruk. . . and to have been a shepherd. . . . In spite of extensive and thorough excavations at Uruk, no contemporary inscriptions are yet known for Gilgamesh or for Lugalbanda. Precise dates cannot be given for the lifetime of Gilgamesh, but they are generally agreed to lie between 2800 and 2500 B.C. Another tradition of parentage for Gilgamesh. . . [states that his father] was a lillu (a man with demonic qualities), and a high priest of Kullab, which is a part of Uruk. . . . The city [of Uruk], which Gilgamesh and his father ruled, is firmly identified as modern Warka, in central Iraq. Excavations by German archaeologists have shown that it was enormously important in the late fourth millennium B.C., with an elaborate central complex of monumental architecture. The city originally consisted of two separate towns on either side, probably, of a canal. . . . In one town the chief, patron deity was the sky god An (or Anu); in the other it was Inanna (Ishtar), the goddess of love and war.

These ancient Mesopotamian cylinder seals bear images of Gilgamesh and Enkidu.

tle, he quenches his thirst at the watering place. With wild beasts he satisfies his need for water.[4]

It was not long before the people living in the villages on the outskirts of Uruk caught sight of this wild man roaming the nearby grasslands, and word soon reached the city. Gilgamesh himself heard about Enkidu and decided to lure the stranger to Uruk and civilize him. The king accomplished the first part of the plan by sending a beautiful woman out into the wilderness. She found Enkidu, who, just as Gilgamesh had expected, fell for her good looks and considerable charms. She convinced the wild man to return with her to Uruk.

The Greatest Wrestler Meets His Match
In the months that followed, Enkidu lived in Gilgamesh's palace in the city. The king's female servants and companions delighted in cutting the wild man's hair, dressing him in fine clothes, and teaching him table manners and other civilized customs. And indeed, fulfilling Gilgamesh's goal, Enkidu slowly but steadily became civilized.

However, Gilgamesh had not counted on this unusual stranger becoming more civilized than the king himself. This happened because the goddess Aruru had instilled in Enkidu a stronger sense of right and wrong than that possessed by the king. One night Gilgamesh invited Enkidu to go for a walk through the city with him and some other companions. When the king was about to enter a house without being invited (perhaps to force himself on another young woman), Enkidu barred his way. He insisted that it would be best if the king did not enter. Instead, he said, the two should continue on their walk.

15

Gilgamesh was angry at being told what to do by one of his subjects, and a terrible fight ensued: The king and Enkidu wrestled each other in the street, crashing into walls and breaking doorposts into showers of splinters. As modern mythologist Norma Goodrich describes it,

> Red with anger, Gilgamesh aimed at Enkidu a great blow on the side of the jaw, which was intended to dash him to the ground. He found the blow parried, however, and the two mighty giants grasped each other by the shoulders, with heads close together and muscles straining, trying each one to throw the other. It was the only time in his life that Gilgamesh, the strongest wrestler in all of the world, had ever felt—arm for arm, back for back, thigh for thigh—a strength equal to his own. Surrounded by a breathless throng of courtiers, lit by the flaring red light of torches, the heroes wrestled. Sweat poured from their mighty muscles, but neither one could budge the other.[5]

Indeed, to the surprise of Gilgamesh and those watching the contest, Enkidu had proved the king's equal in strength, fighting skill, and courage.

Because the great wrestling match had ended in a draw, the two mighty men gained much mutual respect and became instant, inseparable friends. Moreover,

Gilgamesh suddenly saw the evil and futility of his old ways and became a model ruler, causing his subjects to cheer and praise him whenever he appeared in public. Clearly, the goddess's plan had worked, for in the process of transforming Enkidu, Gilgamesh himself had been transformed.

Death Claims a Hero

It was clear to all, even to the gods, that these were not ordinary men but heroes. And it was traditional for heroes, owing to their superior strength and virtue, to go forth on quests to right wrongs and help the downtrodden. Shamash, the sun god, formally requested that Gilgamesh and Enkidu set out together on a heroic mission—to kill a monstrous giant named Huwawa (also known as Humbaba). This dangerous creature was terrorizing the land of the Cedar Mountain, which lay many miles to the west of Mesopotamia. The heroes made the long journey to the forest near the mountain and there encountered the fearsome Huwawa. Somehow, the giant had heard that the heroes were coming, for he was ready for them and even knew their names. According to the old Babylonian account,

> Huwawa made his voice heard and spoke; he said to Gilgamesh, "The fool Gilgamesh and the brutish man ought to ask themselves, why have you come to see me? Your friend Enkidu is a small fry who does not know his own

father! You are so very small that I regard you as I do a turtle or a tortoise, which does not suck its mother's milk.... Even if I were to kill you, would I satisfy my stomach? . . . [No, I definitely would not!] So I shall bite through your windpipe and neck, Gilgamesh, and leave your body for the birds of the forest, roaring lions, birds of prey, and scavengers."[6]

The giant's boastful, threatening words turned out to be a rash display of overconfidence, for together Gilgamesh and Enkidu were a truly formidable pair of fighters. In the ensuing battle, the forest reverberated with the deafening sounds of the blows delivered by the three combatants. Eventually, Shamash himself got involved. The god directed some powerful winds to blow through the cedars and these immobilized the monster, keeping him stuck in one spot while the heroes defeated him and cut off his head. Their exciting victory won them the heartfelt thanks of the people of that land, as well as the respect of Shamash, who had proposed the venture.

But another deity turned out to be much less friendly to Gilgamesh and Enkidu. Ishtar, the goddess of love and war, tried to take Gilgamesh as a lover, and when he refused she decided to punish him by unleashing a giant bull on the city of Uruk. The two heroes managed to kill the bull. But this only further angered the goddess, who placed a deadly curse on Enkidu, causing him to fall ill and die. Gilgamesh was devastated and stricken with grief, and a long, mournful lament flowed from his lips. "For you, Enkidu," he said, tears rolling down his cheeks,

This figurine found by archeologists depicts Ishtar, the widely revered Mesopotamian goddess of love and war.

Syria's Cedars Remembered in Legend?

In this excerpt from his informative book about Near Eastern myths, former University of Manchester scholar John Gray suggests a historical basis for the episode in the Gilgamesh epic in which the title character and his friend, Enkidu, trek westward and confront Huwawa, the giant guardian of the Cedar Forest. Such forests, says Gray, did indeed exist in ancient times along Syria's Mediterranean coast.

[The legend of the encounter with Huwawa] probably reflects the historical tradition of long expeditions from Mesopotamia, which has no heavy timber, to Syria, probably rather to the Amanus range in northern Syria than to Lebanon [which was long famous for its cedar forests]. If the description of "the cedar mountain" as "the abode of the gods" is literal, as it may well be, this might indicate specifically Mt. Saphon, twenty miles north of Ras Shamra [on the Syrian coast]. . . . The description of the encounter with Huwawa, however, indicates a volcano: "Huwawa—his roaring is the flood-storm, his mouth is fire, his breath is death!" This, if it indeed denotes a volcano, cannot be a reference to the Amanus [range] or to Lebanon [which have no volcanoes], but . . . it might denote the volcanoes of the Jebel Druze [a cluster of peaks farther inland in southern Syria], known to the Mesopotamians from Arab traders.

I, like your mother . . . will weep. . . . Listen to me, elders of Uruk, listen to me! I myself must weep for Enkidu my friend, mourn bitterly like a wailing woman. . . . My friend was the hunted mule, wild ass of the mountains, leopard of the open country. We who met and [together] scaled the mountain . . . demolished Huwawa the mighty one of the Cedar Forest, now, what is the sleep that has taken hold of you, Enkidu? . . . [See here, elders, that] he cannot lift his head. I touch his heart, but it does not beat at all. . . . I will lay you, Enkidu, on a bed of loving care. . . . Princes of the earth will kiss your feet. . . . I will fill the proud people with sorrow for you. And I myself will neglect my appearance after your death. Clad only in a lionskin, I will roam the open country.[7]

The Journey to the Great Sea

Keeping his word, Gilgamesh went forth into the desert and wandered for many weeks, all the while contemplating the meaning of death. If the valiant and good Enkidu could die, Gilgamesh reasoned, then he too, and all of his loyal and good subjects, and all people everywhere must someday face death. Surely there was some way to keep this terrible fate from coming to pass. Suddenly, Gilgamesh realized what his greatest and most heroic mission must be: to search out the secret of immortality to save humanity from the scourge of death.

The determined king of Uruk felt confident that he knew the best place to begin his quest. Like many other people, he had heard that the gods had given the secret of eternal life to the former king of Shuruppak—Utnapishtim, the "wise one." The problem was that Utnapishtim lived far to the west on an island in the great sea and no human knew the location of that island or had ever traveled across the sea's

surface and lived to tell about it. Such difficulties did not deter Gilgamesh, however. He made a long, difficult, and dangerous journey that consumed many months and finally came to the towering Mt. Mashu, the home of the sun god. The mountain stood between Gilgamesh and the dangerous waters of the great sea. The fastest way past the obstacle seemed to be a tunnel that went clear through the bowels of the mountain.

Unfortunately, the entrance to the tunnel was guarded by an army of creatures that seemed to be half man and half scorpion. These hideous creatures clicked their massive pinchers and bared their

A carved Babylonian seal shows the hero Gilgamesh wrestling various beasts. He was often referred to as "Gilgamesh the wrestler."

razor-sharp teeth to warn Gilgamesh off, but once more he was not easily discouraged. He walked up to the leader of the scorpion-men, bowed deeply, and introduced himself. He needed to pass through the tunnel, he explained, so that he could reach the great sea and complete a mission crucial to all living things, including the scorpion-men themselves. Gilgamesh made it clear that he sought no trouble and did not want to hurt the creatures.

The chief scorpion-man bowed to Gilgamesh in return and said that he sensed that he was part god as well as human. The scorpion-men believed him, therefore, when he claimed to be on a vital quest, and they would not try to stop him from entering the tunnel. But they warned Gilgamesh that no one had ever made it all the way through, for it was much too long and dark, a darkness so dense that one could not see one's own feet in the inky gloom.

After thanking the scorpion-man for allowing him to pass, Gilgamesh gathered up his courage and entered the tunnel. Though it was pitch black inside and very long, as the scorpion-man had warned, the hero kept on moving, feeling the moist, slimy rock walls along the way. After many hours, he managed to reach the other side. There, he found himself in the enchanting, fragrant garden of Siduri, a goddess known for brewing ale and dispensing wisdom. In Goodrich's words,

> Never even in Uruk had he seen a more beautiful sight. Amid pools and flowers stood the holy tree of the gods, the tree of life, covered with all kinds of delicious, scented fruits. . . . Under it lay a profusion [great amount] of precious gems winking and sparkling in emerald light. At the end of the garden was the house of the goddess, and beyond that the blue waters of the sea that no man had crossed, clearer than a mirror, bluer than a sapphire.[8]

At first, Siduri, in her wisdom, tried to convince the visitor that he should go home. The waters around the forbidden island were lethal, she said. And even with the help of Utnapishtim's boatman, she warned that he would never make it past the pointed crags that formed a ring of death around the island. Gilgamesh refused to listen to reason, however, which was, of course, true to his character. He convinced Siduri to lead him to the boatman, and the two men set forth on the open sea.

Survivor of the Deluge

The journey across the dangerous sea took more than a month. All the while, Gilgamesh was careful not to touch the water's surface, for the boatman had insisted that this would bring anyone instant death. At last, they reached the island and the forest of sharp crags that jutted from the water's surface around it. Thanks to Gilgamesh's extraordinary strength, he was able to use long poles to push the boat away from the deadly rocks. A few hours later, after many months of exhausting travel, the brave and persistent man stood on the beach, staring up at Utnapishtim's great house, which stood on a tall bluff overlooking the sea.

Gilgamesh climbed the bluff, entered the house, and confronted Utnapishtim, who had a bald, very wrinkled head, a long white beard, and sat in a large, comfortable chair. The old man seemed to already know who the traveler was and why he had come. What Gilgamesh sought was not granted to all people, Utnapishtim said. The hero started to object, but the old man waved him into silence and proceeded to tell the story of how he had become the only immortal human being. Hopefully, Utnapishtim said, this would help Gilgamesh to understand the tremendous difficulty in achieving eternal life.

Long ago, Utnapishtim explained, he had done humanity a great service. Like his father before him, he had been the king of the city of Shuruppak, in southern Mesopotamia, and certainly had not begun life as a hero and savior. To the contrary, he had been forced to rise to the occasion when the human race was threatened by a catastrophe sent by the gods. The trouble had begun when the powerful storm god Enlil (who was sometimes viewed as the leader or father of all the other gods) became alarmed at a vast increase in the human population. According to an account on a surviving Mesopotamian tablet,

The country was as noisy as a bellowing bull and the God grew restless at their racket. Enlil had to listen to their noise. He addressed the great gods: "The noise of humanity has become too much. I am losing sleep over their racket. Give the order that disease shall break out."[9]

This move reduced the population as Enlil had hoped it would. But in time the humans multiplied once more, and the great god again became upset at their clamor, which was disturbing his quiet existence. He then had the gods send drought and famine to plague humanity, but these catastrophes proved to be no more permanent than disease had been, for the human population, though significantly reduced in number, always ended up replenishing itself.

Finally, Enlil decided that he must wipe out the humans completely with a great flood. Luckily for the proposed victims, however, Ea, the god of wisdom and freshwater, sympathized with their plight and decided to help them behind Enlil's back. Ea approached Utnapishtim and warned him of the coming deluge. The god instructed him to dismantle his house and use the material to construct a large boat. The man should leave his everyday possessions behind and concentrate on trying to save living things in the ark. Put aboard it the seeds of all the living things on the face of the earth, Ea ordered.

The wise Utnapishtim did as Ea had urged and built the ark. "I loaded it with everything there was," Utnapishtim told Gilgamesh (in a surviving version of the story). "I loaded her with all the seeds of living things, all of them. I put on board the boat all my kith and kin. I put on board the cattle from open country and all kinds of craftsmen."[10] No sooner had he completed this task when the destruction began. For six days and seven nights the wind howled, torrents of rain flooded down and covered the land, and millions of people and animals drowned.

Finally, on the seventh day, the storm subsided and Utnapishtim sadly beheld the devastation wrought by the gods. "Silence reigned," he said,

> for all of humanity had returned to clay. The flood-plain was as flat as a roof. I opened a porthole and light fell on my cheeks. I bent down, then sat. I wept. My tears ran down my cheeks. . . . The boat had come to rest on [the top of] Mount Nimush. . . . When the seventh day arrived, I put out and released a dove. The dove went; it came back, for no perching place was visible to it, and it

turned around. [Later] I put out and released a raven. The raven went and saw the waters receding. And it ate . . . and did not turn round.

A drawing of an alabaster sculpture depicts Gilgamesh, who sought out Utnapishtim, survivor of the great flood.

Then I put all [onboard the ark] out to the four winds [i.e., in all directions] and I made a sacrifice to the gods.[11]

The gods' reactions to the salvation of humanity varied. Ishtar was humbled by the event and swore by her colored necklace (i.e., the rainbow) that she would never forget it. Enlil, on the other hand, was angry that Ea had interfered in his plans to destroy the humans. The tactful Ea managed to calm the chief god, however. And to reward Utnapishtim for his heroic deed, Enlil bestowed on him and his wife (but no other humans) the gift of immortality.

A Lesson for All Generations

The gods granted Utnapishtim eternal life as a special gift, the aging man told Gilgamesh after finishing the tale. So it was not possible for all people to acquire immortality. And even if they could, they would not enjoy it, because living for so many centuries was very boring and lonely.

Still, Gilgamesh would not be put off. He managed to persuade the old man to reveal the existence and location of the "flower of youth," which would give eternal life to anyone who tasted it. The flower grew at the bottom of the sea, said Utnapishtim, at such a depth that no mortal person could hold his breath long enough to reach it. However, the old man

did not fully appreciate how far Gilgamesh's strength and courage exceeded that of ordinary mortals. Indeed, the king of Uruk wasted no time in diving into the sea and retrieving the magical flower.

After thanking Utnapishtim, Gilgamesh set out for home. Never once did the hero consider tasting the flower himself, for his only thought was to bestow this marvelous gift on all of his people. After the passage of many months, Gilgamesh was within a few miles of Uruk when he decided to rest beside a small lake. Placing the flower on a rock, he dove into the water to refresh himself after his long, dusty journey.

When Gilgamesh returned to the rock, however, he saw a snake swiftly slithering away, the flower clenched in its jaws. No matter how hard he tried, the man could not find the snake and had to enter his native city empty-handed. The greatest hero of the land had failed in his ultimate quest. Yet he had learned a valuable, if hard, lesson, and in so doing revealed an essential truth to his people and those of all future generations. This truth is that only the gods are immortal; all human beings, no matter how powerful, or good, or brave, must, as the mighty Enkidu had, face death in the end.

In his long trek westward into what is now called the Mediterranean Sea, Gilgamesh had left the familiar surroundings of his native Mesopotamia. He had penetrated mysterious, desolate, and dangerous lands beyond the comforts and safety

New Research Sheds Light on the Deluge

It has long been an assumption among the majority of modern scholars that the deluge, or great flood, described in the *Epic of Gilgamesh* (and also in the Hebrew Old Testament) was based on a real event. The discovery in the early twentieth century of flood debris in the ruins of an ancient Mesopotamian city seemed to add credence to this idea. The most recent theory about the deluge, however, places the event much farther north. Archaeological evidence has shown that around 5600–5500 B.C., Stone Age farmers from the mountainous regions bordering the northern rim of Mesopotamia began migrating southward into the Tigris and Euphrates plains, which were then largely uninhabited. The reasons for this migration are uncertain. But a group of scholars that includes Columbia University scientists William Ryan and Walter Pitman has proposed that the people may have been escaping a natural catastrophe. They point to evidence showing that before the sixth millennium B.C. the Black Sea, located to the north of these mountains, was a large freshwater lake. Today, that sea is joined to the Aegean and Mediterranean Seas via two straits, the Bosporus and Dardanelles, but originally, the Bosporus was blocked by a huge earthen dam and the lake's level was hundreds of feet lower than that of the seas beyond. Geologic evidence shows that in about 5600 B.C. the dam burst and mighty torrents of water rushed into the Black Sea lake, flooding its shores for many miles inland. Because the date of this catastrophic event roughly coincides with that of the initial southward migrations of peoples into Mesopotamia, Ryan and Pitman suggest that these movements were set in motion by large numbers of refugees fleeing their lakeside villages and farms. They also speculate that over time the memory of the disaster gave rise to the Mesopotamian legends of the great flood. Though this scenario remains unproven, enough circumstantial evidence exists to warrant further serious research and discussion.

of human civilization. For the ancient inhabitants of the Near East who told and retold the tale, the hero's failed quest to find immortality was perhaps a lesson: It was better to accept a short life filled with comfort, companionship, and security than risk all to achieve an eternity of privation, loneliness, and uncertainty.

Two Greek Epic Journeys: The Adventures of Jason and Odysseus

The two greatest and most famous epic journeys of Greek mythology are the quest of the Golden Fleece by Jason and the Argonauts and Odysseus's ten-year effort to reach his homeland. These two stories have much in common. First, they each involve a hero who embarks on a long journey on a ship (or ships) and ends up accomplishing a great goal. In the course of this journey, the hero sails through little-known waters, sometimes reaching what are to him the edges of the known world, and experiences many colorful, often dangerous adventures. In addition, he encounters and is directly affected by the gods and other supernatural beings.

These tales also have in common the fact that the time periods in which they supposedly occurred neatly frame the period of the Trojan War. This siege of the prosperous city of Troy, on the northwestern coast of Asia Minor (what is now Turkey), by an alliance of Greek kings was the subject of the *Iliad*, the famous epic poem by the semilegendary bard Homer. The classical Greeks saw it as a real and momentous event in their dim past and dated it to the thirteenth or twelfth century B.C. If the war did indeed occur in some fashion, this dating may be fairly accurate, for archaeological investigation of the ruins of Troy has shown that the city did undergo a siege in the late thirteenth century B.C.

Ancient Greece

Greek areas

Jason's adventures were thought to have taken place in the generation directly preceding the Trojan War. The goal of his quest was to retrieve the Golden Fleece, the extremely valuable golden hide of a magical flying ram. Many ancient writers produced versions of the quest for the Golden Fleece, among them the Greeks Pindar, in one of his *Odes*, and Apollonius of Rhodes, in his almost six-thousand-line epic poem, the *Argonautica*. The Roman epic poet Valerius Flaccus also wrote an *Argonautica* that has survived.[12] By contrast, Odysseus's story sup-

posedly took place directly following the events of the Trojan War. In fact, because Odysseus (whom the Romans called Ulysses) was a prominent player in that conflict, the fall of Troy acted as the springboard for his long search for home (the island kingdom of Ithaca, located off the southwestern coast of mainland Greece). The main primary source for Odysseus's journey is Homer's other great epic poem, the *Odyssey*.

What sets these Greek epic journeys, as well as many other Greek myths, apart from those of other peoples is their strong feeling of reality. Although monsters and magic abound in these stories, they take place in real places and the heroes seem more like real people than superhuman figures. As the late, world-famous mythologist Edith Hamilton pointed out,

> That is the miracle of Greek mythology—a humanized world,

men freed from the paralyzing fear of an omnipotent Unknown. . . . It may seem odd to say that the men who made the myths disliked the irrational and had a love for facts; but it is true, no matter how wildly fantastic some of the stories are. Anyone who reads them with attention discovers

The Argonauts and the Eruption of Thera

It is possible that parts of Jason's tale were based on dim memories of real events. In this excerpt from his book *Lost Atlantis*, scholar J. V. Luce recalls an episode from the homeward voyage of the *Argo*, in which it encounters a giant named Talos near Crete. Luce then relates various details of this legendary episode to the well-documented large-scale ancient eruption of the volcano on the island of Thera, also near Crete.

He [Talos] was made entirely of invincible bronze except for a vein near his ankle covered by a thin membrane. In terror of his missiles [the rocks he was throwing] the Argonauts backed away from the shore, and were about to sail on when Medea announced that she could overcome the giant. She cast a spell on him which had the effect of dimming his vision, and as he was levering up a great boulder to hurl at them, he grazed his ankle on a rocky pinnacle. "Then the ichor [his life force] flowed out like molten lead," and, losing strength rapidly, he fell from his rocky crag "with a terrible crash." Such is the story as told by Apollonius. . . writing in the third century B.C. But the Argonaut saga goes back to the earliest stages of Greek epic poetry, and has often been supposed to reflect early Greek voyages of exploration. . . . What can we make of this bronze warder who hurls rocks at ships trying to sail to Crete? Is he simply a figure of folk-tale and imagination? . . . [Some scholars have] suggested that the figure of Talos embodies an early Greek memory of the Thera volcano. Thera "guards" the northern approaches to Crete which would have been used by the early Mycenaean sailors. His frame of "unbreakable bronze" represents the wall of the newly formed crater on the mountain peak of Thera as it then was. The rocks which he throws are the "bombs" shot from the vent of the volcano. His "heel" is a subsidiary volcano on the coast of the island. . . . He collapses and becomes quiescent when all his ichor has flowed out like "molten lead"—a reminiscence of the cooling off of lava streams after the end of an eruption.

that even the most nonsensical take place in a world which is essentially rational and matter-of-fact. . . . A familiar local habitation gave reality to all the mythical beings. If the mixture seems childish, consider how reassuring and how sensible the solid background is as compared with the Genie who comes from nowhere when Aladdin rubs the lamp and, his task accomplished, returns to nowhere.[13]

A Royal Usurper Receives an Ominous Prophecy

In Jason's tale, the "familiar local habitation," as Hamilton terms it, is the powerful city of Jolcos (or Iolcos) in Thessaly in central Greece. The great quest for the Golden Fleece arose not long after an oracle had delivered a prophecy to the king of Jolcos, Pelias. (An oracle was a priestess in a god's temple who, it was thought, conveyed messages, also called oracles, from that god to humans.) The oracle warned Pelias to beware of any stranger who arrived in Jolcos wearing only one sandal, for this man would cause Pelias to lose both his throne and his life. Because the king had usurped the throne from his uncle, clearly an illegal act, he felt that the prophecy was ominous and worrisome, for it might mean that the gods were angry with him for his crime.

Pelias had good reason to be worried. It

came to pass that just such a one-sandaled man, having lost a sandal while crossing a flooded stream, appeared at the palace. The stranger informed Pelias that he was his cousin Jason, the son of the rightful king. Jason had come to claim his birthright and to bring back enlightened rule to Jolcos, which

In this marble statue copied from a Greek original, the hero Jason holds the object of his famous quest—the fabulous Golden Fleece.

Pelias had administered harshly. Because the two men were kin, Jason did not seek to fight or harm Pelias. Instead, the younger man simply called on the king to do the right thing and step down from the throne. Pelias could keep all the wealth that he had recently accumulated, along with his flocks of sheep and other livestock. But he must transfer the royal crown of Jolcos to Jason, after which Jason would gladly make Pelias the chief royal adviser.

Pelias had to think fast on his feet. He did not want to give up the throne, but he knew he had to find some way to appease this young royal claimant or else risk violence or even civil war. After all, the prophecy had stated that Pelias would lose his life to a one-sandaled man. It seemed logical that the way to keep the prediction from coming true was to avoid getting into a fight with Jason. So the king deviously pretended to agree with Jason's claim to the throne, but secretly he plotted to rid himself of the young man. Jason would indeed become king of Jolcos. First, however, he had to accomplish a special task that would prove to the people that he was worthy of ruling them.

Jason grasped the hilt of his sword and promised gladly to perform any task that Pelias named. Smiling, Pelias told him that he was continually vexed by a spirit who bade him to bring the fabulous fleece of the legendary Golden Ram back to Jolcos, its rightful home. At the moment, the Golden Fleece hung in a tree in the faraway land of Colchis, and since Pelias was too old and weak to make the journey, Jason must do so. When the young man returned with the fleece, Pelias said, swearing by Father Zeus, he would willingly abdicate and make Jason king. This was another lie, of course. Pelias knew full well that the voyage to Colchis was long and extremely treacherous and that in all likelihood Jason would never return.

Preparations for the Voyage

As for Jason, he never even considered the idea that he might never come back. Indeed, he was confident that he could bring back the Golden Fleece, which would, through its magical properties, bring good fortune to the city and its people. However, to succeed in this endeavor, Jason realized he would need a special ship. Under the direction of the goddess Athena, the master shipbuilder Argus came to Jolcos to construct the mighty *Argo*. According to Valerius Flaccus's account,

A large gathering of men worked busily. At the same time . . . a grove of trees had been felled on all sides and the stores were resounding with the steady blows of the double-edged ax. Already Argus was cutting pines with the thin blade of a saw, and the sides of the ship were being fitted together. . . . Planks [were] being softened over a slow fire until they bent to the proper shape. The oars had been fashioned

The Argo, carrying the hero Jason and his intrepid crew, sails toward the distant land of Colchis in search of the fabulous Golden Fleece.

and Pallas Athena was seeking out a yardarm for the sail-carrying mast. When the ship stood finished, strong enough to plow through the pathless sea . . . Argus added varied ornamental paintings.[14]

Such a superior ship needed a superior crew, and Jason soon gathered together many of the strongest, ablest, and noblest men of Greece. Among their number was the mighty hero Heracles (whom the Romans called Hercules), the strongest man in the world and a renowned warrior and monster killer. He was accompanied by his faithful armor-bearer Hylas. "In the first bloom of youth," says Apollonius in his account, Hylas "went with Heracles to carry his arrows and serve as keeper of the bow."[15] Other prominent Argonauts included the master musician and singer Orpheus; the warrior Peleus (father of Achilles, who would become the most famous hero of the Trojan War); and Zeus's twin sons, Castor and Polydeuces (the Roman Pollux).

Finally, there was the matter of who should be the commander of the expedition. Jason felt that this honor should go to the strongest and most valuable man in the crew and called on the men to choose that champion. According to Apollonius,

The young men's eyes sought out the dauntless Heracles where he sat in the center, and with one voice they called on him to take command. But he, without moving from his seat, raised his right hand and said: "You must not offer me this honor. I will not accept it for myself, nor will I allow another man to stand up. The one who assembled this force must be its leader

too." The generosity that Heracles had shown won their applause and they accepted his decision.[16]

The Initial Adventures

After choosing their leader and storing sufficient provisions for the voyage, Jason and his Argonauts finally embarked and sailed north. It was not long before they encountered their first setback, which took place near a bay where they had stopped for rest and exercise. As the noted nineteenth-century classical scholar Charles Kingsley told it,

Heracles went away into the woods, bow in hand, to hunt wild

What Kind of Ship was the Argo?

In this excerpt from his classic book *The Ancient Mariners,* noted scholar Lionel Casson describes a fighting ship that was common in early Greek times, the kind of vessel the classical Greeks likely envisioned the *Argo* to be when telling and retelling the myth of the Golden Fleece.

The Argo could not stay at sea any length of time. Roomy merchantmen [large cargo ships] that could stay long at sea were being built in this age, but the Argo was not one of these. Jason wisely chose a fighting ship for his expedition, one which would not be so completely dependent upon the winds as would a sailing freighter and which could either withstand or run away from attack. His vessel could not have been very different from those used in the war against Troy: a slender ship mounting twenty-five rowers on a side, with a sail and mast that could be easily and quickly dismantled. When traveling without a break night and day, the crew slept at their oars and there was little room for provisions. Frequent stopovers had to be included in the itinerary.

deer; and Hylas the fair boy slipped away after him, and followed him by stealth, until he lost himself among the glens, and sat down weary to rest himself by the side of a lake; and there the water nymphs came up to look at him, and loved him, and carried him down under the lake to be their playfellow, forever happy and young. And Heracles sought for him in vain, shouting his name till all the mountains rang; but Hylas never heard him down under the sparkling lake. So while Heracles wandered searching for him, a fair breeze sprang up, and Heracles was nowhere to be found; and the *Argo* sailed away, and Heracles was left behind.[17]

Thus, Heracles missed the Argonauts' subsequent adventures. These included narrowly making it through a channel bordered by the dreaded Clashing Rocks, which perpetually smashed together and destroyed anything caught between them, and passing perilously near the country of the Amazons (daughters of Ares, god of war), a tribe of fierce women warriors. They also sailed past the great rock on which the ancient god Prometheus lay chained and heard the flapping of the wings of the eagle that plagued him. (Prometheus had stolen fire from heaven and given it as a gift to humanity. As a punishment, Zeus, the leader of the gods, had ordered that Prometheus be chained to a great rock and that a giant eagle should come each day and gnaw at his insides.)

In one particularly exotic and dangerous episode, the Argonauts tangled with the terrifying Harpies, flying creatures endowed with pointed beaks and claws and a sickening stench.[18] One evening the Argonauts came ashore on the European coast of the Bosporus (one of the two narrow channels that divide the Aegean and Black Seas). There, they found an old man named Phineus, who was so starved and emaciated that all that was left of him was quite literally skin and bones. Jason asked what had happened to the poor fellow, and Phineus answered that Apollo, the god of prophecy and light, had granted him the gift of prophecy. However, Zeus did not like the idea of humans knowing what he was going to do next, so he inflicted a punishment on Phineus. Every time the man began to eat a meal, the Harpies, whom some people called "Zeus's Hounds," would swoop down and either steal his food or cover it with their vile stench, making it too disgusting for him to eat.

Jason and his men decided to help Phineus. Two of the Argonauts, Zetes and Calais, were the sons of Boreas, the North Wind, so they possessed the ability to fly through the air, which gave them the best chance in a fight against flying creatures like the Harpies. Jason and the others gathered up a huge amount of food and prepared a magnificent banquet for Phineus. Meanwhile, Zetes and Calais stood on either side of the old man, their swords drawn and ready in case the Harpies appeared. Sure enough, as Apollonius told it,

> Phineus had scarcely lifted the first morsel [of food], when, with as little warning as a whirlwind or a lightning flash, the Harpies dropped from the clouds proclaiming their desire for food with raucous cries. [Before the warriors could react], the Harpies had devoured the whole meal and were on the wing once more, far out to sea. All they left behind was an intolerable stench. . . . Raising their swords, the two sons of the North Wind flew off in pursuit.[19]

In this eighteenth-century engraving, the Argonauts rescue poor old Phineus from the Harpies, seen fleeing at upper right.

Eventually, Zetes and Calais caught up to the disgusting creatures. And the men would surely have cut them to pieces if the goddess of the rainbow, Iris, had not intervened. Iris was a sister to the Harpies and sought to protect them. She told Zetes and Calais that if they did not kill the Harpies, she would promise to keep them away from old Phineus. The two warriors spared the creatures, and Iris did indeed keep her word, so thereafter Phineus was able to eat his fill without harassment. Jason and his men continued on their voyage to faraway Colchis, taking with them some valuable advice from Phineus about the potential dangers that lay ahead.

Facing More Dangers in Colchis

After several months of travels fraught with dangers, Jason and his crew reached the land of Colchis, on the far end of the

Black Sea, where they were to face still more dangers. They asked the local king, Aeetes, to give them the Golden Fleece; in exchange, they would do him some important service such as fighting his enemies. Aeetes, however did not like foreigners, and in any case, he was not about to give up the fleece, so he concocted a plan that would surely result in Jason's death. No one could take the Golden Fleece, Aeetes claimed, unless he first proved his courage through a formidable challenge. He would have to gain control of two fearsome fire-breathing bulls, yoke them, and then make them pull a plow. That plow would create furrows into which Jason would throw dragons' teeth; once planted, these seeds would quickly grow into a multitude of armed warriors whom he would have to defeat.

At first, it seemed to Jason that no mortal man could pass such a test. But he soon received some unexpected and formidable aid. The goddess Hera, Zeus's wife and protector of marriage, wanted Jason's quest to succeed. She convinced the love goddess, Aphrodite, to send her own son Eros (the Roman Cupid) to Colchis. Eros caused King Aeetes' daughter Medea to fall in love with Jason almost instantly, and her love became so strong that she was willing to betray her own father for this Greek stranger. Medea, who possessed knowledge of sorcery, met Jason in secret and gave him a vial containing a magic drug. In Apollonius's version of the story, she gave Jason these instructions:

In the morning, melt this charm, strip naked, and using like an oil, rub it all over your body. It will endow you with tremendous strength and boundless confidence. You will feel yourself a match, not for mere men, but for the gods themselves. Sprinkle your spear and shield and sword with it as well; and neither the spear-points of the earthborn men, nor the consuming flames that the savage bulls spew out will find you vulnerable.[20]

Sure enough, covered in this special ointment, Jason was able to yoke the bulls, defeat the seed warriors, and thereby pass the test. Aeetes still did not want to give up the fleece. But with more help from Medea, Jason managed to get past the huge serpent that guarded the fleece and to spirit the prize out of Colchis and bring it back to Greece.

Revenge of the Goddess

After returning to Greece, the mighty band of Argonauts disbanded. Some of the heroes went on to further adventures of their own. Others had sons who, when they grew into young men, joined the great Greek expedition against Troy that ended with that city's destruction. Even though the Greeks were victorious in the war, thanks in large degree to the help of various gods, many never made it back from the Trojan shores that had been their home for ten long years. The principal cause of this misfortune was an act of sacrilege against a prominent goddess. While the Greek soldiers were sacking the city, they went on a rampage, and during the commotion one of them broke in to the local temple of Athena, the goddess of war and wisdom. The intruder dragged away the Trojan king's daughter Cassan- dra, who had invoked the goddess's protection by throwing her arms around her statue.

Athena was determined to make the Greeks pay for this outrage. She convinced the sea god Poseidon, who had sided with the Greeks during the war, to help her mete out their punishment. He proceeded to produce a tremendous storm that struck the Greek fleets as they were sailing homeward from Troy. The tempest was so violent that Agamemnon, king of Mycenae, lost many of his ships; Menelaus, king of Sparta, was blown off course and ended up in Egypt; and hundreds of Greek sailors drowned.

Having slain the serpent, which lies dead at his feet, Jason reaches for the Golden Fleece, as Medea and Orpheus (one of the Argonauts) look on.

One of the Greek leaders, though, suffered much longer than the others. Wily Odysseus, king of Ithaca, was condemned to wander to many distant and exotic places, and it was ten full years before he saw the shores of his native island again. In the tenth year of his travels, shortly before he made it home, Poseidon, who was still angry with him, wrecked the raft on which he was floating and Odysseus washed ashore in the land of a friendly people called the Phaeacians. The Phaeacian king, Alcinous, threw a banquet for the visitor, who told his host the story of his

The Trojans and Greeks battle furiously. Odysseus, one of the heroes of the war, was forced to wander for ten years following its conclusion.

eventful and perilous ten-year journey.

"For nine days I was chased by those accursed winds across the fish-infested seas," Odysseus began, as Homer told in the *Odyssey*. "But on the tenth day we made it to the country of the Lotus-eaters, a race that live on vegetable foods."[21] The local inhabitants, he went on, gave some of his men some potent flower-food, which made them feel lazy and forgetful and lose their desire to continue homeward. Odysseus finally had to resort to

dragging these men back to the ships and chaining them to keep them from remaining forever in Lotus Land.

Outwitting the One-Eyed Giant

Next, Odysseus recalled, "we came to the land of the Cyclopes, a fierce, uncivilized people, who never lift a hand to plant or plow, but put their trust in Providence." The Cyclopes' society is very different from that of civilized peoples, the storyteller explained. They "have no assemblies for the making of laws, nor any settled customs, but live in hollow caverns in the mountain heights, where each man is lawgiver to his children and his wives, and nobody cares a jot [the least bit] for his neighbors."[22]

Because the one-eyed Cyclopes were so uncivilized, and very large and powerful, the Greeks wanted to avoid contact with them. But Odysseus's men needed food, so he took twelve of them ashore. It was not long before they found a huge cave in which many sheep and goats were penned. But before the men could gather up the animals and depart, the Cyclops who lived in the cave returned home. This crude giant, Polyphemus, barred the entranceway with a gigantic rock. When he asked where the strangers had anchored their ship, Odysseus shrewdly answered that it had been wrecked in a storm and that he and his companions were the sole survivors. Polyphemus then abruptly grabbed two of the Greeks, smashed them on the rocky floor until they were dead, and gulped them down for his supper.

The next morning, the Cyclops killed and ate two more of Odysseus's men and then left for the day, securing the great rock in the doorway so that the Greeks could not escape. When the giant returned that evening, he made still another meal of two men and then began to guzzle wine. In time, he demanded to know the Greek leader's name. Giving another shrewd reply, Odysseus claimed his name was "Nobody."

Later, the Cyclops fell asleep and Odysseus and his remaining men sharpened a wooden beam and heated it in the fire. Lifting the pole, Odysseus recalled, he and his men

> drove its sharpened end into the Cyclops' eye, while I used my weight from above to twist it home, like a man boring a ship's timber with a drill. . . . In much the same way we handled our pole with its red-hot point and twisted it in his eye till the blood boiled up around the burning wood. The fiery smoke from the blazing eyeball singed his lids and brow all round, and the very roots of his eye crackled in the heat. . . . He gave a dreadful shriek, which echoed round the rocky walls. . . . He pulled the stake from his eye . . . and raised a great shout for the other Cyclopes who lived in neighboring caves along the windy heights.[23]

When the other giants appeared outside the cave and asked Polyphemus what was wrong and who was hurting him, he remembered the name Odysseus had given him and called out, "Nobody!" Hearing that "nobody" was hurting their neighbor, the other Cyclopes, confused and a bit irritated, returned to their homes.

Pig-Men and the Spirits of the Dead

The next morning, the blinded Polyphemus had to roll back the huge rock to let his animals out to graze, and this allowed the Greeks to make their escape. The enraged Cyclops cried out to his father—who, unfortunately for Odysseus, happened to be Poseidon—to punish these men who had deceived and disfigured him. Poseidon gladly did so.

As a result, Odysseus continued to wander for many years, encountering numerous adventures and misfortunes along the way. These included falling into the clutches of a race of giants, who ate all of his men except the crew of his own flagship; stopping at the isle of Aeaea, where the sorceress Circe changed half of his remaining men into pigs; and sailing past the isle of the Sirens, deadly sisters whose deceptively lovely singing lured humans to their deaths.

Odysseus also journeyed to the edge of the underworld, the dark world of the dead, and attempted to consult the spirit of a dead wise man to find the way to

Odysseus and his men pierce the single eye of the giant Cyclops Polyphemus. Unfortunately, Polyphemus turned out to be Poseidon's son.

Ithaca. But when the hero sacrificed some sheep to invoke the spirit, the souls of hundreds of other dead people rose up and surrounded him. The eerie horde included "fresh brides," Homer wrote,

> unmarried youths, old men with life's long suffering behind them . . . and a great throng of warriors killed in battle, their spear-points gaping yet and all their armor stained with blood. From this multitude of souls. . . there came a moaning that was horrible to hear.[24]

ODYSSEUS ATTACKING CIRCE   ETRUSCAN MIRROR NEW YORK

The back of an ancient Italian mirror shows Odysseus confronting the sorceress Circe.

Among the wailing spirits were some of Odysseus's own men who had died during his recent adventures, and also his mother, whose presence moved him to tears. In addition, the ghost of the mighty warrior Achilles, whom Odysseus had known well in life, appeared. The two veterans of the war at Troy spoke and, through the sad and surprising words that left the dead man's lips, Odysseus learned a great truth about life and death. Achilles had been the strongest of the Greeks, Odysseus said, and the most formidable and fortunate of all men. Now that he was in the underworld, Odysseus believed, Achilles must be a virtual prince among the dead, for surely even death could not vanquish him. The pale ghost of Achilles spun around and let out a discontented howl. It cried out to Odysseus to cease his praise of dusky death. If he could return to the earth, the ghost said, he would gladly work as a laborer for some poor, luckless fellow. Though it might sound like a miserable existence, it would be infinitely better than being king of the dismal, lifeless underworld.

Odysseus was so dismayed by his encounter with the spirits that he gathered his men and fled back out onto the open ocean. There, they encountered a tremendous gale that killed all in the party except Odysseus himself. He ended up in a cave on a distant island ruled by the nymph (minor goddess) named Calypso, who kept him there for seven years. Finally, Zeus took pity on him and ordered her to release him. And it was not long afterward, Odysseus told his listeners at the banquet, that he had reached the Phaeacians' friendly shores.

How the Gods Are Depicted in the *Odyssey*

Here, from her history of ancient Greek literature, scholar Jacqueline de Romilly discusses the manner in which Homer portrays the Greek gods in his epic poems. This portrayal was important, for the later Greeks derived much of their conception of the gods from it.

[Homer] imagined the gods as living on Mt. Olympus, or simply in the sky. Their king and father was Zeus; but each had his or her own distinct personality. The poet imagines their relations with one another as those that might exist in a small human kingdom. . . . Like men, these gods have passions. . . [that] often lead them to mingle with men, sometimes in their proper shapes, sometimes in disguise. They have their friends and their enemies. . . . With all these characteristics, the Homeric gods are not merely anthropomorphic [possessing human form and attributes] but "human" in the extreme, with all the failings the word implies. Yet they are also radically different from men, for they are immortal and enjoy superhuman powers. . . . The gods transform themselves freely; and they transform men as well, making them old or beautiful at will—not to mention the more drastic metamorphoses [transformations] of which the Odyssey offers several examples (notably Circe's transformation of men into pigs). . . . Homeric man is always afraid that a god may be present to thwart him. . . . [Yet] the close ties between gods and mortals can also lead to a kind of affectionate familiarity—at least in the Odyssey. If Odysseus is hounded by Poseidon's anger, he is just as constantly helped by Athena, who is always acting in his behalf, either among the gods, or in Ithaca, or wherever he is.

An imaginary drawing of Homer. No one knows his true appearance.

The End of the Quest— Home

After a short stay with the Phaeacians, Odysseus was delighted when King Alcinous offered to help him return to his beloved island of Ithaca. But when, after ten long years of trials and tribulations, he landed there, he found his palace and family sorely troubled. Because most Ithacans assumed that Odysseus had long since died, his faithful wife, Penelope, was beset by over a hundred suitors. Each of them wanted to marry her for the money and titles he would get. After an emotional reunion with his now grown son Telemachus, Odysseus, disguised as a beggar, entered the palace banquet hall where the suitors were gathered. There, he revealed himself to the startled men, and aided by Telemachus and two loyal servants, in a rage he began to fight and kill them. Homer dramatically described the death of one suitor, Eurymachus, this way:

> He drew his sharp and two-edged sword of bronze, and leapt at Odysseus with a terrible shout. But at the same moment the brave Odysseus let an arrow fly, which struck him by the nipple on his breast with such force that it pierced his liver. The sword dropped from his hand. Lurching across the table, he crumpled up and tumbled with it, hurling the food and wine-cup to the floor. In agony he dashed his forehead on the ground; his feet lashed out and overthrew the chair, and the fog of death descended on his eyes.[25]

The nymph Calypso, pictured here, kept Odysseus captive on her island for seven years.

Eventually, all of the suitors lay dead in the blood-soaked room.

With the honor of their royal house restored, Odysseus and Penelope were finally reunited. During the twenty years they had been apart, both had been forced into situations in which they had to employ considerable cunning and resourcefulness. They had also displayed great perseverance and loyalty; both had never stopped believing that they would be reunited in their marriage bed, which Odysseus had long ago built himself using a live olive tree as one bedpost. When, at long last, they held each other again, they were so overwhelmed with joy that they both shed tears. To prolong this touching scene for the lovers, Athena stretched forth her hand to delay the coming of the dawn. And in the following days, all hearts in Ithaca were filled with joy.

Odysseus had encountered many bizarre and marvelous beings and locales during his ten years of wandering, sights that many adventurers would pay dearly to see. But all the while he had known in his heart that he was no adventurer; instead, his inner being was grounded in the simple, mundane, but emotionally fulfilling reality of his home and family. Unlike the epic journeys of many other heroes, his quest had not aimed at reaching fabulous faraway places. In fact, it was just the opposite: His goal was to make it home. And for the rest of his life, he could rest content that he had achieved his goal.

The Journey of Aeneas, Father of the Roman Race

The major mythical quest of the ancient Romans was also their greatest, proudest founding legend. The story of Aeneas, a Trojan prince who journeyed to Italy and there established the Roman race, was committed to writing in the first century B.C. by the incomparable Roman poet Virgil. And this magnificent epic poem, the *Aeneid*, remained Rome's national epic.

One is immediately struck by the fact that the Trojan War, from which the character Aeneas derived, is the major epic myth of the Greeks rather than the Romans. Why did the Romans turn to the Greeks for inspiration in so important a matter as their very identity as a people? The answer is not hard to fathom considering the development of ancient Roman culture. Generally speaking, the Romans were great imitators who skillfully adapted the best customs and ideas of neighboring peoples and tailored them to their own needs. The first-century B.C. Roman historian Sallust described this talent of his ancestors, saying,

> [they] were never too proud to take over a sound institution from another country. . . . In short, if they thought anything that an ally or an enemy had was likely to suit them, they enthusiastically adopted it at Rome; for they would rather copy a good thing than be consumed with envy because they had not got it.[26]

More than any other people, the Greeks served as cultural models for the Romans, and Greek religious, artistic, and literary ideas profoundly influenced all aspects of Roman life. For example, numerous Roman gods became Romanized versions of Greek deities, as in the case of the Roman Jupiter, originally an Italian sky god, who came to be associated with Zeus, the supreme leader of the Greek gods. (The merging of Greek and Roman culture is referred to as "classical" civilization.)

More specifically, like all peoples in all ages, the ancient Romans wanted to believe that they were descended from characters of heroic stature. And their mythology, like that of the Greeks, was crowded with heroes who had performed valiant deeds in bygone eras. However, when the early Romans first came into contact with Greek culture, they became painfully aware that their own ancient heroes did not quite compare in stature with some of those of the Greeks. In particular, the Romans had no equivalent of the Trojan War, which was not only dramatic, but emphasized humans' glorious deeds and the interaction between humans and the high gods. So, the Romans simply borrowed part of the Trojan myth and made it their own. At least by the sixth century B.C., it appears, Roman legends had incorporated the tale of Aeneas's escape from the burning Troy and his fateful journey to Italy. As for how this blatant adoption of a Greek tradition squared with Roman pride, the noted classical scholar T. J. Cornell comments,

> In general it is not surprising that the Romans were willing to embrace a story that flattered their pride by associating them with the legendary traditions of the Greeks,

whose cultural superiority they were forced to acknowledge— albeit sometimes grudgingly. More specifically, in Greek myth Aeneas possessed qualities which the Romans liked to see in themselves, such as reverence for the gods and love of his fatherland. The Trojan legend was also useful to the Romans in that it gave them a respectable identity in the eyes of a wider world, and one that could be used to [their] advantage in their dealings with the Greeks. . . . Finally, we should note that by claiming to be Trojans the Romans were saying that they were not Greeks, and in a sense defining themselves in opposition to the Greeks. . . . In the hands of Virgil and other writers of the first century B.C. it became a means to reconcile them, and make Roman rule acceptable in the Greek world.[27]

Aeneas Recalls the Fall of Troy

Aeneas's fateful story certainly gave the Romans a respectable identity in the eyes of many of the peoples they encountered and conquered. As told in Virgil's *Aeneid*, the tale begins seven years after the fall of Troy. The Trojan prince's small fleet of ships was plying the calm waters near the large Mediterranean island of Sicily when the

Virgil's Epic and Rome's Destiny

Composed in Latin between 29 and 19 B.C. by the poet Virgil, Rome's greatest epic poem, the *Aeneid*, tells the story of Rome's national hero and founder of the Roman race, the Trojan prince Aeneas. The author intended for the work to celebrate Rome's origins and achievements, as well as to glorify the person and accomplishments of his friend Augustus, the first Roman emperor. Virgil had not quite finished the poem when he died in 19 B.C.; his colleagues Varius Rufus and Plotius Tucca edited it on his behalf. The work is notable not only for the skill and nobility of the writing, but also for its unapologetic conception of the Romans as having a divine destiny to rule the world. Virgil portrays all of Roman history as a continuous narrative leading up to a preordained and inevitable outcome—the accession of Augustus, the "child of the Divine," and the advent of the Roman Empire, which will lead the world into a golden age of peace and prosperity. As the late historian R. H. Barrow put it in *The Romans*, "The most significant movement of history . . . according to Virgil, is the march of the Roman along the road of his destiny to a high civilization; for in that destiny is to be found the valid and permanent interpretation of all [human] movement and all development. . . . The stately *Aeneid* progresses throughout its length to this theme, the universal and the ultimate triumph of the Roman spirit as the highest manifestation of man's powers."

An eighteenth-century depiction of the Roman poet Virgil.

goddess Juno (wife of Jupiter) intervened. With her divine powers, she could foresee the awful possibility that Aeneas's descendants might destroy her favorite city, the lovely and prosperous North African metropolis of Carthage. (This turn of events actually occurred many centuries later when the Romans defeated the Carthaginians in the three devastating Punic Wars.) So she mustered up a violent storm, hoping to scatter and destroy Aeneas's vessels. According to Virgil,

The winds . . . swirled out and swept the land in a hurricane, whirled on the sea and whisked it deep to its bed, from every quarter hurling the breakers [waves] shoreward. . . . From Trojan sight, darkness descended on the deep, thunder shackled the poles, the air crackled with fire, everywhere death was at the sailor's elbow. Terror played fast and loose with Aeneas's limbs and he moaned and lifted his arms to the stars in prayer. . . . The waves towered to the stars; the oars were smashed, the bow yawed . . . and a huge mountain of toppling water battered the vessels' beams.[28]

When the tempest finally subsided, Aeneas and his surviving followers made their way to the nearest shore, which, as fate would have it, turned out to be the coast near Carthage. The men entered the city and soon Aeneas met its queen, Dido, who fell madly in love with him. (This happened partly because Venus, the Roman equivalent of the Greek love goddess Aphrodite, willed it. She was Aeneas's mother, who had mated with a mortal man—Anchises, of the royal house of Troy—to produce him, and she wanted Aeneas to stay in Carthage.) As Dido got to know the Trojan prince, "his noble blood and state," Virgil wrote, "his face and his voice were branded upon her breast, forbidding sleep."[29]

This painting by eighteenth-century French artist Pierre Geurin, shows Aeneas recounting his exploits to Dido in her city of Carthage.

At a great banquet in the Carthaginian court, Dido begged Aeneas to describe his recent adventures to her and her noble courtiers. She implored the brave soldier to tell them about the end of that mighty city, Troy, and how he had escaped its flames carrying his aged father, Anchises, on his back. In Norma Goodrich's telling of the tale,

> Silence fell on the assembled guests. All turned toward the god-like Aeneas, who spoke from his couch. "Unspeakable is the grief you ask me to recall for you, how the Greek swept over our lofty walls and laid in dust the proudest city of Asia. I was there. I saw it all happen." Aeneas covered his eyes with his hand and bowed his head. After a pause he began again, "yet, if you wish to hear the death agony of our civilization, if your love for the Trojans urges you to inquire into such an appalling disaster, although my very soul shudders to recall it, I will begin."[30]

Aeneas proceeded to tell his listeners how his brother, Hector, the greatest Trojan champion, had been slain by the mighty Greek warrior Achilles. Then, after having besieged the city for ten years, the Greeks suddenly offered the Trojans a token of peace—a huge wooden horse. But this was only a ruse. After the Trojans, thinking the war was over, dragged the supposed gift into the city, a band of Greek warriors hiding

Aeneas carries his aged father, Anchises, on his back while fleeing Troy in this early modern painting.

inside the horse crept out and opened the gates for the rest of their army. The victors went on a killing spree and torched the city. Meanwhile, Aeneas explained, he and some close kin and followers managed to escape. Having lost their home, they had no other choice but to search for another, so they built some ships and set out into the blue-green waters of the Aegean Sea.

A Journey Guided by Prophecies

The Trojan refugees, Aeneas continued, made one of their initial stops at the tiny sacred island of Delos, which lies at the center of the Aegean. There, an oracle gave Aeneas a message from Apollo, the god of prophecy and healing. The Trojans should seek out their "ancient mother," the message said, the land from which their distant ancestors had originally come. But Aeneas and his companions had no idea where this ancient motherland might be, and the oracle had given no substantial clue. Thinking that it might be the island of Crete (which lies southeast of the Greek mainland), Aeneas led his followers there. But after they had landed, they received another message from Apollo, this one informing them (according to Virgil):

Since Troy was consumed [by fire], we [i.e., the gods] have followed you and your arms. We have been with you through every . . . crest of ocean your fleet has weathered, and we shall raise your prosperity to the stars and give to your city its mighty sway. . . . You must move your habitation—it was not these shores that [I] commended [to you]. . . . There is a place the Greeks have called Hesperia—the western land—an ancient country powerful in war and rich of soil. . . . [The inhabitants call] themselves

Aeneas and his followers attempt to drive away the loathsome Harpies in this painting by French artist François Perrier.

"Italians" after Italus—one of their leaders. There lies your true home.[31]

In this way, Aeneas learned that his fate was to sail to Italy to establish a new home for his people.

If only the voyage to faraway Italy had been a quick and easy one, Aeneas told Dido and the others. With a heavy sigh, he explained how instead it turned out to be a long, complicated, and dangerous venture. Sailing westward into the larger reaches of the Mediterranean, the Trojans stopped on one of a group of islands known as the Strophades. No sooner had they slaughtered some cattle, cooked the meat, and settled down for a meal, when a flock of Harpies appeared seemingly out of nowhere. These hideous, smelly, birdlike creatures, which had large sharp claws and women's faces, descended on the gathering and fouled the food by covering it with their sickening stench. Aeneas and his followers managed to drive the creatures away, but the retreating Harpies uttered a combination of prophecy and curse. Aeneas would make it to Italy, they said, but he would not be allowed to establish a walled city of his own until hunger had driven him to devour his tables. (When Aeneas and his followers later sailed up the Tiber River in Italy, they stopped to eat and were so hungry that after finishing their meal they ate the thin bread-cakes they were using as platters; Aeneas interpreted these as their "tables"

and concluded that the Harpies' prophecy had been fulfilled.)

After the Harpies had departed, Aeneas continued westward, constantly harassed by the goddess Juno, who still harbored resentment toward him and the other Trojans. The travelers soon came to the shores of Epirus (in extreme northwestern Greece). And there, to their great surprise, they found that the ruler was Helenus, a Trojan and one of Aeneas's kinsmen. Helenus was also gifted with the ability to see into the future. Taking Aeneas aside, he told him that the gods had fated that he would succeed in his great quest, but only if he did certain specific things to help overcome the obstacles along the way. First, said Helenus, Aeneas should avoid a channel bordered by dangerous falling rocks. (This was one of the same danger spots that the Greek king Odysseus had encountered during his own perilous journey following Troy's downfall.) Second, after reaching Italy, Aeneas must seek out and get the advice of a renowned local priestess and prophetess, the Sibyl. And third, a great city would eventually rise on a riverbank where Aeneas would see a white sow and her thirty babies resting.

Dido's Rage

Thanking Helenus, Aeneas gathered his followers and once more sailed toward the setting sun. Although the travelers managed to avoid the dangerous rocks Helenus had warned them about, they made the mistake of stopping on an uncharted island to gather provisions. There, they came on a bedraggled old Greek. Claiming to be one of Odysseus's men who had been left behind accidentally, he informed them that this was the land of the Cyclopes, the frightening one-eyed giants. Moreover, Polyphemus, the Cyclops whom Odysseus and his men had blinded, lived nearby. "He is hideous to look on," said the Greek (according to Virgil),

> nor can his mind be moved by human speech. He feeds on the entrails [insides] and the dark blood of his unhappy victims. With my own eyes I have seen him snatch up two of our number in his colossal hand and brain them on a rock. . . . I have seen all the floor awash with spurting blood. I have seen him crunch their limbs up dripping with dark blood and their joints warm and twitching still as his jaws closed over them.[32]

Only seconds later, the subject of this grisly tale, the giant Polyphemus, appeared and threatened Aeneas and his band. Luckily, the Trojans managed to elude the creature's clutches and make it to the shore of Sicily (which lies just south of the Italian peninsula). However, their happiness at having escaped a gruesome death was now overshadowed by an unexpected bout of grief. Anchises, Aeneas's father, by now very frail and exhausted by the arduous trek,

died, leaving his son and the others weighed down by a heavy sadness.

After leaving Sicily, Aeneas said, finishing the story of his adventures, a terrible storm struck and drove the Trojans to the beaches of Carthage—and to their meeting with their goodly host, Dido. The queen was delighted with the tale and now even more in love with Aeneas than she had been before. She begged him to stay with her and make Carthage, rather than Italy, his new home. The Trojan prince came to care deeply for Dido, and for a while it looked as though he might forget about his prophesied Italian destiny and become the king of the North African kingdom she ruled.

However, mighty Jupiter did not desire for Aeneas to settle down in Carthage. The leader of the gods sent his messenger, the swift-footed Mercury, to remind Aeneas that he had a duty to future generations of Italians. "You forget, it seems, your true kingdom, your destiny!" Mercury told Aeneas (in Virgil's account of the story).

> Now Jove [another name for Jupiter] Almighty, the absolute monarch of the gods, has sent me, he who holds heaven and earth in the palm of his hand. . . . What are you doing? Why do you linger here in north Africa? If no ambition spurs you, nor desire to see yourself renowned for your own deeds, what about Ascanius [Aeneas's son]? The realm of Italy and the Roman inheritance are his due.[33]

Hearing this appeal, Aeneas came to his senses and prepared to leave Carthage. Not surprisingly, Dido was both grief-stricken and angry that Aeneas would suddenly leave her this way; and despite her love for him, she hurled harsh words at him. "You traitor!" she screamed.

"Did you hope to mask such treachery and silently slink from my land? Is there nothing to keep you? Nothing that my life or our love has given you, knowing that if you go, I cannot but die? . . . Why, if Troy still stood, would you seek Troy across these ravening waters? Is it unknown lands and unknown homes you seek, or is it from me you flee? You see me weep. I have nothing else but tears and your right hand to plead with. . . . If you ever found in me any sort of sweetness, pity me now! . . . If prayer has any potency [strength] change your mind!". . . [When he refused to change his mind, she screeched,] "Oh God, I am driven raving mad with fury! . . . Go! Seek Italy on a tempest, seek your realms over the storm-crests, and I pray if the gods are as true to themselves as their powers that you will be smashed on the rocks, calling on Dido's name![34]

Then she pronounced a terrible curse. May future Carthaginians and Aeneas's descendants always hate one another, she

A depiction of the god Mercury, whom Jupiter sent to remind Aeneas about his destiny.

said. Let there be no treaties between the two peoples and let generation after generation be consumed by weapons and war. Soon afterward, as Aeneas's ships sailed from Carthage's harbor, the livid, grieving queen grasped a sword and plunged it into her breast, ending her life.

Italian Landfall

After departing Africa, Aeneas and his company sailed back to Sicily, arriving about a year after old Anchises had died there. The local ruler welcomed the travelers and helped them to stage some athletic games to honor Anchises. During the celebration, the Trojan women mourned the loss of their homes and loved ones years before in Troy.

Meanwhile, the goddess Juno was secretly watching. She still wanted to thwart Aeneas's plans to reach Italy so she hatched a sinister plan designed to force

him and his followers to remain in Sicily. She sent down the rainbow-goddess, Iris, disguised as one of the grieving Trojan women. Iris gathered the women around her and told them that their unhappiness over losing their homes was perfectly understandable. Aeneas had only prolonged their agony and that of their poor children, she said, by refusing to stay in one place. For

Who Was the Real Roman Founder?

As noted scholar Jane Gardner points out in this excerpt from her book *Roman Myths,* the story of Aeneas founding a parent city of Rome on the Latium plain was only one (although the most popular) of many alternative Roman founding legends. Some myths claimed Aeneas established Rome itself, while others attributed the deed to various descendants of his.

Already in the late sixth century B.C., the story of Aeneas's flight from Troy was known in Etruria [the homeland of the Etruscans, north of Rome]; it is depicted on a number of Athenian black-figure vases found there. The motif [theme] also appears on . . . statuettes found at the Etruscan town Veii and on Etruscan gems. He is first associated with Rome by Hellanicus, a Greek historian in the fifth century B.C., who wrote that Aeneas founded Rome and called it Rhome . . . after one of the Trojan women accompanying him. Some Greek writers, however, ascribe the foundation not to Aeneas but to other Trojans and Greeks; in one version, Rome was founded by a son of [the Greek wanderer] Odysseus and [the sorceress] Circe. Later Aeneas reappears, as father or grandfather of the founder of Rome. . . . There was an alternative tradition, that Rome was founded, not by Aeneas or any Trojan or Greek founder, but by Romulus and Remus. Some early Roman historians said that they were Aeneas's sons, or grandsons. However, it came to be realized that Aeneas, or even his grandchildren, really would not do as founders of Rome. When a Greek scholar, Eratosthenes of Cyrene (275–194 B.C.) . . . fixed a date of 1184 B.C. for the fall of Troy, the length of the gap between Aeneas and Romulus became obvious. Various dates, ranging from 814 to 728 B.C., were proposed for the foundation of Rome; the one which eventually became accepted was 753 B.C. [and a long line of kings was inserted, which] conveniently filled the gap [between Aeneas and] the birth of Romulus and Remus, and, some years later, the foundation of Rome.

years he had forced them to wander from one end of the great sea to another, passing up many opportunities to establish new homes in friendly, pleasant climates. Aeneas's followers should put a stop to this nonsense, she said. The ruler of this fair land of Sicily had welcomed them and they should accept his hospitality and make their new home there, where they knew it was safe, rather than continue on to unknown and potentially dangerous lands. Having said all this, the disguised goddess incited the women to light torches and burn the ships. Then, she exclaimed, Aeneas would have no choice but to give the order to stay.

When the women, roused to anger by the words of the disguised goddess, began to burn the ships, Aeneas was horrified. He cried out to mighty Jupiter, saying that if the ships were destroyed, his people would lose the will to go on. And in that case the great mission the chief god had foreseen for Aeneas and them would never come to pass. Hearing this plea, Jupiter sped through the sky, towing some huge, dark storm clouds, which soon released torrents of rain that doused the fires. Most of the ships were saved. But four were beyond repair, and because of a lack of room in the surviving vessels, Aeneas decided to leave the crews of the lost ships, along with their families, to make new homes in Sicily.

The two groups of Trojans said their tearful good-byes. Then, guided and protected by Venus, who kept a wary eye out for Juno, Aeneas crossed from Sicily to Italy, making landfall near Cumae, on the peninsula's southwestern coast. This location was no random choice. Indeed, Cumae was the home of the Sibyl, the wise woman and seer whom Aeneas's kinsman, Helenus, had instructed him to find and consult.

The Sibyl and the Descent into the Underworld

Aeneas made his way to Cumae's impressive Temple of Apollo and arranged an audience with the Sibyl, who, he learned, lived in a deep, forbidding cavern near the temple. After entering the cavern, the Trojan leader found the woman sitting on a rock and dressed in a black robe that covered most of her body. She greeted him as if she knew him (since, being a prophetess, she was well aware of who he was and why he had come) and bade him to sit down. She had communicated with the gods about him, she said. And in their view he had done well in making it this far. Moreover, if Aeneas remained steadfast in his courage and resolve, he would make it farther. The fair and fruitful plain of Latium, which lay many miles north of Cumae, awaited him, the Sibyl said. It was there that he should attempt to establish a kingdom. However, he should be warned that the goddess Juno still opposed him, so his path was still littered with potential dangers. Among those dangers that the prophetess could foretell, he was destined to fight a bloody war over the right to marry an Italian bride, and he would have to engage in a fight to the death with a warrior nearly as formidable as Achilles, who had slain Aeneas's valiant brother Hector before the towering walls of Troy.

Aeneas's eyes went wide and then he sighed, for this new and momentous information was a great deal to absorb and sort out. He thanked the priestess for her insights and prevailed on her for one other favor. He asked her to find him a way into the underworld so that he might once more see his beloved father, who had died during the long journey across the sea from Troy. The Sibyl not only granted the man's request and told him how to find the entrance to the realm of the dead, she also accompanied him in his quest to find the spirit of old Anchises.

Descending into the darkness, Aeneas began to see the souls of people both long

The ghastly boatman Charon ferries Aeneas and the Sibyl across the River Styx.

and recently dead. There were ghosts of old people who had been fortunate enough to have lived long lives, and also those of infants, still crying for their mothers left behind on earth. But saddest of all for Aeneas was his unexpected encounter with a pale, thin form that he recognized as the spirit of Queen Dido, who had loved him so. "The tears rose to his eyes," Virgil wrote,

> and in soft loving tones he said to her: "Oh Dido, unhappy one, was the story true that was brought to me? They told me you had used a sword to end your life. . . . I swear by the stars, by the gods above . . . it was not of my own desire that I left your land. Oh Queen, it was the inexorable [inescapable] bidding of heaven. . . . Do not withdraw yourself from my sight, I beg you! . . . These are the last words I shall ever speak to you; fate allows me no more.". . . But she, with her head averted, and eyes fixed on the ground. . . flung herself away and fled into the shadows.[35]

Shocked and grieved at Dido's unjust fate, Aeneas, still accompanied by the silent Sibyl, continued on until he found his father. Following their joyful reunion, the old man offered to reveal the future of the grand and blessed race Aeneas would sire. "Come, my son," said Anchises, "I shall show you the whole span of our destiny." First, he said, Aeneas would build a city on the plain of Latium, south of the Tiber River. Later, his offspring would establish the city of Alba Longa in the same region, and the line of Alba's noble rulers would lead to a young man named Romulus, who himself would establish a city—none other than Rome. "Under his tutelage," Anchises predicted, "our glorious Rome shall rule the whole wide world, and her spirit shall match the spirit of the gods."[36] Anchises showed his son a vision of the long line of noble Romans, finally culminating in the greatest of them all, Augustus Caesar, who was destined to bring about a new golden age for Rome and humanity. (Indeed, it was Augustus who established the Roman Empire.)

The War with the Latins

After Aeneas and the Sibyl returned from their journey through the underworld, the hero traveled northward to Latium to fulfill the destiny that had been revealed to him. He journeyed up the Tiber River, where he saw a white sow and her piglets on the riverbank, just as the prophet Helenus had foretold he would. And nearby he met villagers living on the Palatine Hill (the future site of Rome). Aeneas also met the local ruler of Latium, Latinus, and soon sought the hand of that king's daughter, Lavinia. But Turnus, the prince of a neighboring people called the Rutulians, had already asked for Lavinia's hand, and the

Aeneas slays the Latin prince Turnus, thereby winning the hand of the princess Lavinia.

rivalry over Lavinia soon led to a terrible war, thus fulfilling the Sibyl's prophecy that Aeneas would fight over an Italian bride.

The war dragged on and on as the Trojans fought an alliance of local Latin peoples organized under Turnus. Eventually, Aeneas and his leading opponent faced each other in single combat, much as Achilles and Hector had at Troy. And in this way, another part of the Sibyl's prophecy came to pass. "Aeneas mounted his chariot and drove into the battle," as Norma Goodrich tells it.

From a distance, Turnus heard him come. . . . All were hushed to see those two brave men, born in opposite ends of the earth, come up against each other in a battle to the death. The mobs of soldiers drew back. Latins moved over to make room for the Trojans they had been trying to kill the minute before. . . . And like two bulls they met, Aeneas and Turnus, horn to horn and shield to shield, struggling for footing, swords flashing and then locked to the hilt, forehead to forehead. . . . Blow after blow they landed until the blood flowed from a hundred cuts. Then Turnus lifted his sword in what he hoped would be the final stroke, but Aeneas caught the blow glancing on his shield, and the weapon broke.[37]

At a fatal disadvantage, Turnus pleaded for Aeneas to spare him. But the Trojan champion, angry over the lack of mercy his opponent had shown others in the war, killed him, ending the conflict.

Afterward, Aeneas established a city in Latium, naming it Lavinium after Lavinia, whom he married. And from the union of the Trojan and Latin races, fulfilling the destiny ordained by Father Jupiter, sprang the lineage of the noble Romans, who would one day rule the known world. For the Romans, Jupiter had earlier told Venus, "I see no measure nor date, and I grant them dominion without end. Even Juno . . . will mend her ways and vie with me in cherishing the Romans, the master race, the wearers of the toga. So it is willed!"[38]

Aeneas ended up fulfilling all the prerequisites for a hero on an epic quest. He had a noble, difficult goal, one that would require him to make a long journey to an unknown and potentially hostile land. He also encountered monsters, human adversaries, and numerous other dangers along the way. Finally, he came face to face with and benefited from magic and spiritual forces in the form of the gods, the Sibyl, and the ghosts of the underworld. All of these factors made Aeneas a noble and larger-than-life character. And it is no wonder that the Romans retold his story often and with great pride.

Celtic Quests: The Search for Love and Perfect Morality

Though the epic quest is a common theme in mythology, for some unknown reason the Celts had more tales of heroic quests than most ancient peoples. Among the most important and prolific of Europe's early inhabitants, the Celts were originally a seminomadic tribal people. They spread across large portions of the continent between 1200 and 100 B.C.; and at their maximum extent, between around 400 and 200 B.C., they occupied Ireland and Britain, most of France and Spain, and large portions of central Europe stretching eastward to the western shore of the Black Sea.[39]

Unlike the Mesopotamians, Greeks, and Romans, the Celts long lacked written literature. This had a direct bearing on how their myths were eventually transmitted to later ages. Because they did not record their traditions, myths, laws, and other ideas in

writing, the original Celtic myths passed from generation to generation by word of mouth. The first literary references to the Celts and to Celtic gods and myths were those of the classical Greek and Roman writers. Their narratives are fascinating and important, but since these writers were biased by their contempt for a people they viewed as "barbarians," they often presented a distorted view of their subjects.

More important written sources of Celtic mythology are those that were composed in the early Irish and Welsh tongues from roughly the sixth through the twelfth centuries. Although these sources are much more informative and reliable than the Greco-Roman ones, they also present some formidable problems. First, they contain mainly the legends of the Celts of that region, so they leave out the surely extensive and rich lore of the rest of Celtic

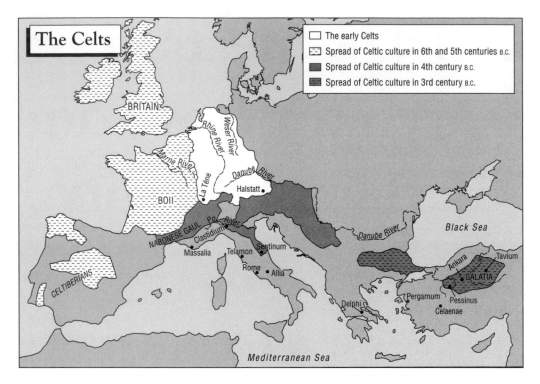

Europe. Second, they were written during the medieval Christian age that directly followed the disintegration of the classical Greco-Roman world. Most of the compilers were Christian monks who felt obliged to make many of the old pagan myths more "acceptable" to Christian readers, so they often reduced pagan gods to human historical figures or presented the myths as collections of childish superstitions rather than as integral facets of a different and equally worthy religious system.

A later, final category of sources for Celtic mythology consists of a number of late medieval Welsh and English romances. Many of them deal with the legendary English ruler King Arthur, one of the greatest and most popular heroes in world mythology and folklore. According to Philip Wilkinson,

The mythical King Arthur, famed as Briton's brave and virtuous leader, was probably based on a real person. He may have been a British leader in the Dark Ages, just after the Romans left Britain in the fifth century. During medieval times, different writers . . . wrote about Arthur, retelling the ancient myths about the Knights of the Round Table, who met at Arthur's court at Camelot. They chronicled his chivalry, told of the events leading to his death, and looked to the time when the "once and future king" would rule again, presiding over a golden age.[40]

Among the more important medieval sources dealing with Arthur and his knights are English (or Welsh) chronicler Geoffrey of Monmouth's *History of the Kings of Britain*; tracts by Frenchman Chrétien de Troyes and Englishman Thomas Malory; and a long anonymous work, *The Quest of the Holy Grail*, dating to about 1225. The search for the Holy Grail, or Sangreal (supposedly the cup used by Jesus Christ during the Last Supper), was undertaken by several of Arthur's knights. Only Sir Galahad, however, proved morally pure enough to actually hold the fabulous artifact in his hands and through it to enter Christ's embrace. The tale remains one of the two or three most memorable and often retold tales in the entire genre of epic quests.

The Coming of Sir Galahad

The immediate events leading up to this memorable quest for the cup of Christ began when King Arthur received a message from his old mentor and friend, the magician Merlin. The old seer had given the message to one of the king's most trusted knights, Sir Gawain, who had delivered it to Camelot. As Arthur knew well, Gawain said, quoting Merlin almost word for word, the Lord Jesus once drank from the Grail, so it was a sacred object with special powers of healing. Long ago, Joseph of Arimathea, the kind man who provided the tomb for Jesus after the crucifixion, brought the Grail to Britain. For many years, it was displayed

One of the many early modern paintings depicting Jesus at the Last Supper. His cup, the Holy Grail, rests on the table before him.

in a church for the faithful to come and view and draw inspiration from. But one day the man who was then guarding the cup proved himself unworthy of the honor. He looked with lustful eyes at one of the young female pilgrims who was praying before the Grail, and in an instant the miraculous object vanished from sight, causing all of those present to despair. Thereafter, the Grail remained somewhere in Britain, hidden away. Only in a less sinful time, when a person of truly pure heart and soul should seek it out, would its blessings fall once more on the people of this land. That time, Gawain said, had finally arrived. The man destined to find the Grail was alive at that very moment, and Arthur would soon meet him. Merlin's message concluded by urging the king to support the holy endeavor in any way he could.

Excited by Merlin's words, Arthur wondered how he might discern the identity of the person destined to seek out the Grail. That information came to him in a way he did not anticipate. Camelot was preparing its annual celebration of the Pentecost (a feast commemorating the seventh Sunday after Easter, when Christ appeared to the Apostles). When the Pentecost feast began, all the noble knights and ladies who had

The Grail—Both a Christian and Celtic Symbol

In this excerpt from his book about Celtic mythology, scholar Arthur Cotterell explains that the Holy Grail was a powerful Christian symbol. Yet it also bore traits and powers reminiscent of Celtic cauldrons. These mythical and mystical containers were said to provide food and wealth, to bring the dead back to life, and/or to dispense wisdom.

That the Grail was the representation of the body and blood of Christ there can be no doubt. . . . There remains, nevertheless, a powerful charge of Celtic magic in this Christian myth. When the Holy Grail, covered with a white cloth, appeared at Camelot, the vessel filled Arthur's hall with the most tasty smells, so that the knights of the Round table ate and drank as never before. It was, in fact, nothing less than a Celtic cauldron of plenty. When, at the end of the Quest, the Grail became Christ's body, the draft that Sir Galahad took from it at Joseph of Arimathea's request ensured his spiritual survival. Like a Celtic cauldron of rebirth, it allowed Sir Galahad to live on in a Christian otherworld [similar to the otherworlds of Celtic mythology, where heroes resided after leaving earth]. This obvious debt to Celtic mythology meant that the Church never fully embraced the Grail as a Christian symbol. The great popularity of the Grail stories forced a degree of toleration [by Church authorities], but clerics were always aware of its links with pre-Christian rites.

gathered in the castle's great hall witnessed a singular, wondrous event. As described in the anonymous *Quest of the Holy Grail,*

> There came a clap of thunder so loud and terrible that they thought the palace must fall. Suddenly the hall was lit by a sunbeam which shed a radiance through the palace seven times brighter than had been before. . . . Not one of those present could utter a word, for all had been struck dumb. . . . When they had sat a long while thus, unable to speak and gazing at one another like dumb animals, the Holy Grail appeared, covered with a cloth of white. . . . Yet no mortal hand was seen to bear it. . . . It circled the hall along the great tables and each place was furnished in its wake with the food its occupants desired. When all were served, the Holy Grail vanished, they knew not how or whither.[41]

After the vision had ended, Arthur and his guests regained the power of speech, and the hall was abuzz with excited conversation about what had just transpired. All agreed that the kingdom had been given a special honor and that Christ had given a sign that the time had come for men of goodness to seek out the Grail. Gawain suddenly cried out that he would gladly go on a quest for the sacred cup. He would leave the next day and not rest until he had found it.

Sir Galahad and his horse rest in a glade during the relentless quest for the Holy Grail.

Numerous other knights sprang to their feet and offered similar vows. Arthur was troubled, for he realized that losing so many of his strongest knights to such a quest would break up the mighty fellowship of the Round Table, which he had labored so long to achieve.

Before the king could muse further, he heard a new flurry of voices and saw that everyone was looking toward the front of the hall. An old hermit was leading an extraordinarily handsome young man through the crowd and toward the throne. What did the hermit want, Arthur asked, and who was the young man who stood beside him? The hermit answered that the young man was a knight named Galahad, who was the son of Sir Lancelot, one of the bravest of Arthur's knights. At this, the hall was again abuzz until Arthur waved for silence. Galahad had been raised by his mother at the court of his grandfather in France, the hermit continued, and he had come to Camelot to prove his worth as a knight of the Round Table.

Requesting that everyone watch closely, the old man led Galahad around the great Round Table to a conspicuously vacant chair. This was the so-called Seat of Danger, which had always sat vacant, waiting for a knight who would be pure enough of heart and mind to recover the Grail. Every man who had dared to sit in the chair had been instantly swallowed up by the earth, never to be seen again. But to everyone's astonishment, Galahad sat in it without ill effect. Seeing this, Arthur, with a touch of awe in his voice, declared that Galahad was welcome in Camelot. Indeed, the seat had apparently long been waiting for the young man, its rightful owner, to arrive.

American painter Edwin Austin Abbey's version of Galahad approaching the Seat of Danger.

The Shield and the Cross

But Galahad was not destined to occupy his seat at the Round Table for long, for, as many other knights had earlier, he now pledged to go in search of the Grail. In a sad voice, Arthur told his assembled knights that he feared that this might be the last time he would see them all together as a fellowship of brave comrades. He requested that the following day they have one last tournament and joust together to celebrate that fellowship. The next morning, all the knights met in the jousting area in a meadow near the castle. "The queen and all her ladies had mounted the walls," says *The Quest of the Holy Grail,*

and Galahad, who had ridden out into the meadow with the rest, began to aim his lances with a force and fury that astonished all the onlookers. He accomplished so much in so short a space [of time] that there was not a man or woman present but marveled at his exploits and accounted him victor over all comers. And those who had never seen him before said that he had made a worthy beginning in the way of chivalry, and that if his feats that day were proof, he would easily surpass all other knights in prowess. Indeed, when the tournament was over, it was found that of all the companions of the Round Table bearing arms that day there were only two that he

had not unhorsed, and those were Sir Lancelot and Sir Percival.[42]

Not long after the tournament, Galahad, Gawain, Percival, and several other knights set out, each in a different direction, to seek the Holy Grail. Of all these valiant men, only Galahad bore no shield. He had heard a story about a very special shield that lay in an abbey several days' ride from Camelot, and he hoped to acquire this prize before continuing the quest. When he reached the abbey, Galahad entered, and a holy man showed him the shield, which had a large red cross painted on it. The shield was waiting for its rightful owner to come and claim it, the holy man told him. And so far, all those who had taken it from the abbey had met with defeat or disaster.

Galahad soon witnessed this process for himself. A foreign knight, King Bagdemagus, arrived to claim the shield, and moments after taking it from the abbey, he found himself challenged by a mysterious knight dressed completely in white armor. As Galahad watched, the white knight raised his lance and attacked Bagdemagus, easily wounding and unhorsing him. As the white knight rode away, a squire returned the shield to the abbey.

Soon afterward, Galahad entered the abbey, took the shield, and followed the tracks left by the white knight's horse. It was not long before the two formidable knights were face to face, and Galahad asked whether the other man was going to attempt to unhorse him. The white knight answered that he would not. This mighty shield, he explained, had once belonged to Joseph of Arimathea, the same good man who had brought the Grail to Britain. It had rested in the abbey for centuries, waiting for the last of Joseph's line to come and claim it and go forth with it to find the Grail. Having said this, the white knight wished Galahad good luck in his quest and then vanished, seemingly into thin air. Now realizing that he was a kinsman of the Grail's first guardian, Galahad continued on his way, bearing the shield with renewed confidence.

Because of past sins, Sir Lancelot (left), one of King Arthur's most formidable knights, was not destined to see the Holy Grail.

Percival Meets a Woman in Distress

Meanwhile, as the months passed, the other knights who had set out to find the Grail did not fare well. Sir Gawain realized that he was not pure enough of mind and spirit to be worthy of seeing the sacred cup, and so he lost heart and returned to Camelot. Lancelot, though uncommonly brave, also proved unworthy. This was because he had engaged in an illicit love affair with Arthur's wife, Guinevere, and the moral stain of that mistake could not be erased. So Lancelot lost his way during his journey and was not one of those who were privileged to see the Grail.

As for Percival, one day he was riding through the forest when he came to a bridge over a small river. A group of twenty or more mounted soldiers guarded the bridge, and when the lone knight requested passage, they asked who he was. Hearing that he was one

Another Abbey painting shows Sir Galahad battling the seven knights who had attacked his colleague, Sir Percival.

of Arthur's followers, they attacked him, for they served one of Arthur's enemies. Percival was able to kill the first two men who came at him, but then seven others struck him simultaneously and unhorsed him. He would surely have been killed had a knight carrying a large shield embossed with a red cross not appeared and lent him aid. Percival cried out a greeting as he recognized his Round Table comrade Sir Galahad. Like some force of nature, the younger knight

smashed into the remaining attackers, scattering them. Then he began picking them off one by one, piercing their armor and chests with his lance, until the last few gave up and fled.

Percival was thankful for Galahad's help, but greatly perplexed when his fellow knight did not stop to talk with him. Instead, Galahad rode away into the forest, as if he was so driven by the need to fulfill the quest that he could not waste precious time on mere pleasantries. Disappointed, Percival found his horse, continued on his way, and soon came to the sea. There, he saw a small ship at anchor not far offshore and a lovely woman rowing toward him in a skiff. The two introduced themselves. The woman said that she had been a very rich woman until a cruel lord disinherited her and threw her out to fend for herself. Since that time, she had been traveling from place to place seeking a champion with the courage to help her regain her good name and position.

Ever ready to aid a damsel in distress, Percival offered to help the woman. He boarded her ship and soon found himself so strangely drawn to her that he forgot about the holy quest he had undertaken. That night, she lured him to her bed, and he was just about to climb in to it when he glanced at his sword lying on the floor. The red cross it bore on its hilt reminded him of his duty

Boarding the Miraculous Ship

The following scene, from the anonymous thirteenth-century work *The Quest of the Holy Grail*, describes Galahad, Percival, Percival's sister, and Bors boarding the mysterious and miraculous ship bearing the Grail.

They made their way in single file to where they saw the ship. On their approach they found it more magnificent by far than the one they had left; but they were most amazed at seeing no soul on board. They drew nearer in the hope of making some discovery, and looking at the ship's side they saw an inscription . . . which bore a dire and alarming message to all intending to embark; and it ran thus: "Give ear, O person who would set foot in me. Whoever you are, take heed that you be full of faith, for I am faith itself . . . and as soon as you lapse from faith, I'll cast you down in such a way that you will find in me neither help nor footing.". . . [Percival's sister said to him,] "I warn you, as a person I hold most dear, on no account to step aboard this ship if you do not have perfect faith in Jesus Christ, for in doing so you would bring about your death forthwith. For the ship is so sublime a thing that none who bears the taint of vice can stay aboard it safely." Hearing this, Percival. . . embraced her joyfully and said to her, "In truth, fair sister, I will go aboard; and shall I tell you why? So that, were I to prove no true believer, then might I die a traitor's death, and if I am strong in faith and such as a knight should be, I may be saved." "Then enter in safety," she replied, "and may Our Lord be your defense and safeguard." While she was speaking, Galahad, who was standing in front, raised his hand to bless himself and stepped aboard. . . . The maiden followed him in, making the sign of the cross as she entered. Seeing this, the other two hesitated no longer, but went on board as well.

to the quest, and he made the sign of the cross on his forehead. Instantly, the ship evaporated into a cloud of black smoke, leaving the knight stranded on the beach. The woman, now revealed as an evil enchantress, screamed and angrily cursed at her failure to seduce Percival, then herself dissolved into smoke and evaporated into the sky.

Journey to the East

Several more months passed. Galahad was still searching relentlessly for the Grail, but each time he felt that the sacred object was close at hand he found that he was mistaken. One day a young woman sought him out and asked him to follow her, saying that he would be rewarded with the greatest adventure of his life. Intrigued, the knight went with the woman, who led him to the seashore. There, Percival and another of Arthur's knights, Sir Bors, were waiting for him.

After the men greeted and embraced one another, Galahad asked the other men why they had sent for him. Did they have some new insight that might lead them all to their goal—the sacred cup? Indeed they did, Percival answered. The young woman who had led Galahad to this place was Percival's sister, and she had experienced a vision in which she had seen the four embark on the ship that was anchored in the nearby harbor. Furthermore, she was convinced that the ship would lead the searchers to the Grail and their destiny.

Hoping that the woman's vision had been sent by Christ, the four pilgrims boarded the ship and sailed away. Eventually they came to a huge whirlpool that blocked their way through a narrow channel. Floating nearby was another ship, and Percival's sister urged her companions to board it, saying that it would take them safely beyond the obstacle that confronted them. This prediction proved accurate, for once the four boarded the second vessel, it lurched forward and sped clear over the dangerous whirlpool. The ship then continued on, racing across the sea's surface toward the east, as if driven by some powerful, unseen force. This was indeed the case, for it soon became clear to Galahad and the others that the wondrous object they sought—the Holy Grail itself—was onboard the vessel with them. They could not yet see it, but they could feel its presence beneath a red cloth atop a table made of pure silver.

For more than two weeks, the ship carried its four awestruck passengers eastward, far beyond Britain. They passed through the Pillars of Hercules (the Strait of Gibraltar), skirted south of the island of Sicily, and continued on until the shores of the Holy Land came into view. Disembarking, the four visited the holy city of Jerusalem, hoping to receive divine guidance. They told the story of their quest for the Grail to the local king. But when they said that they had been borne across the sea by the power of the object itself, the king decided they were liars and impostors and locked them away

Sirs Galahad, Percival, and Bors near the end of their quest in this famous painting by English painter Dante Gabriel Rossetti.

in his prison. For a full year they languished in that deep, dark hole. Then the king fell ill. He came to believe that he had wronged the four strangers, and on his deathbed he released them and asked for their forgiveness, which they gave him only minutes before he died.

The city was now without a king. And the people, who had by now heard about Galahad's unusual goodness and purity, begged him to rule over them. Reluctantly, he accepted this offer and asked Percival and Bors to stay on as his advisers. They agreed to do so. The new king installed the silver table bearing the still-covered Grail near the altar of a chapel, where the three knights, Percival's sister, and others came daily to pray in the presence of the special object.

Galahad's Fate

Things remained this way for exactly one year. On the anniversary of the day Galahad had become king, the three knights entered the chapel to say their usual prayers and noticed a strange old man standing next to the silver table. The man gestured to Galahad and told him it was time for him to look beneath the cloth and see the object he had devoted much of his life to find. As written in *The Quest of the Holy Grail,*

> Galahad drew near and looked at the Holy Grail. He had but glanced at it when a violent trembling seized his mortal flesh at the contemplation of the spiritual mysteries. Then lifting up his hands to heaven, he said: "Lord, I worship you and give you thanks. . . . You have fulfilled my wish to let me see what I have ever craved, and I pray that now you will allow

me to pass from earthly life to life eternal."[43]

The old man lifted the Grail and handed it to Galahad, who held it with the greatest care and respect and drank from it. Then the man revealed that he was Galahad's ancestor Joseph of Arimathea. The Lord had assigned him this task because he, like Galahad, was morally pure enough to be worthy of handling the Grail.

Feeling the end of his earthly life nearing, Galahad turned to Percival and Bors and embraced them in a tearful farewell. Then, Galahad suddenly slumped to the

Galahad finally comes face to face with the Holy Grail—as depicted in Edwin Austin Abbey's magnificent painting.

floor and, as his companions watched in awe, a great band of angels appeared and bore the young man's soul upward toward heaven. No sooner had this occurred when a huge hand, glowing with an unearthly brilliance, passed straight through the wall, grasped the Grail, and disappeared with it. When Percival and Bors looked around the room, they saw to their amazement that Joseph of Arimathea had also vanished.

Percival was so strongly affected by what he had witnessed that he laid down his sword and lance and entered a local monastery. He died there about a year later. As for Bors, he buried Percival, made his way back to Britain, and told King Arthur about what had transpired in the years since he and his companions had left Camelot. Hearing this inspiring tale, Arthur ordered that it be set down in writing and kept in the library at Salisbury. Future generations must know of these wonders, he declared.

Culhwch's Quest for the Hand of Olwen

The search for the Grail was not the only quest undertaken by members of Arthur's court. Culhwch, the son of Cildydd, a knight of the Round Table, went on a renowned quest for the love of a woman. The circumstances leading to this adventure began when Culhwch, who was also King Arthur's cousin, was just a boy. When Culhwch was very young, his mother died and his father soon remarried. His stepmother came to hate the boy and she placed a curse on him, saying that the only woman Culhwch would ever love would be Olwen, the daughter of Ysbaddaden. This was a terrible curse because Ysbaddaden was an extremely ornery one-eyed giant who would sooner die than allow his daughter to marry an ordinary man (even though Olwen was herself an ordinary woman). Thus, poor Culhwch was destined to spend his whole life pining away over a woman he could never have.

Culhwch grew to young manhood unaware of the curse that his stepmother had inflicted on him. One day, however, on hearing Olwen's name for the first time, he fell madly in love with her (which was part of the curse), and he decided that he must seek her out and marry her. His father suggested that he go to Camelot and ask for Arthur's assistance, which Culhwch did. Two of Arthur's knights, Cei and Bedwyr, agreed to accompany the young man on his quest for the hand of fair Olwen.

The three warriors journeyed overland for almost a year until they reached the towering castle in which Olwen and her monstrous father dwelled. The wife of a local shepherd arranged a meeting between Culhwch and Olwen, who, hearing that a handsome young suitor had arrived, slipped quietly out of the castle. Soon, Culhwch gained his first glimpse of the woman of his dreams. According to the *Mabinogian*, an ancient Welsh romance,

> She arrived wearing a robe of flame-red silk about her, and around her neck a choker of red gold imbedded

with precious pearls and rubies. . . . Whiter was her flesh than the foam of the wave. . . . Whiter were her breasts than the breast of the white swan. Redder were her cheeks than the reddist foxgloves. Who so beheld her would be filled with love for her.[44]

Culhwch proceeded to tell Olwen of his desire to marry her. And because she was immediately taken with the well-spoken young man, she accepted his proposal. However, she explained, her father was against any such marriage. So, Olwen said, Culhwch must go to him and ask for her hand, and he must agree to perform any tasks her father demanded of him. Otherwise, she would not agree to the marriage.

Culhwch agreed to follow Olwen's instructions. But when he and his companions approached Ysbaddaden the next day, the giant flew into a rage and hurled spears at them. The men dodged the missiles and succeeded in hurling them back, wounding Ysbaddaden. The same thing occurred when the three men called on the giant the next day. On the third day, Ysbaddaden let loose his spears again, and this time when Culhwch threw one back it struck the giant in the eye. Ysbaddaden screamed and accused Culhwch of being a savage. This was no way for a would-be son-in-law to treat a prospective father-in-law, the giant said.

Culhwch countered that it was the giant who had resorted to violence first and then

In costume and appearance, Culhwch likely resembled this Celtic warrior.

loudly demanded Olwen's hand in marriage. To this, Ysbaddaden replied that he was the only one who could make demands in that land, and if Culhwch wanted to marry his daughter he must first complete a series of tasks. Only if all of these demands were met, and to the letter, would the giant grant his permission for the marriage.

Culhwch, whose love for Olwen left him no choice but to agree, found the tasks assigned by the giant extremely difficult and exhausting. There were thirty-nine of them; the most dangerous of all was to steal a comb, razor, and scissors from between the ears of Twrch Trwyth, a monstrous wild boar that roamed the forests of Ireland, and to return them to Ysbaddaden. King Arthur himself aided Culhwch in tracking Twrch Trwyth, a chase that took months and led them all over Ireland.

When all of the tasks had been completed, Culhwch and another knight, Goreu, went to Ysbaddaden. And as told in the ancient text,

> Culhwch asked, "Is your daughter mine now?" "She is," the giant answered. "But don't thank me for it. Instead, thank Arthur and his men, who won her for you. I would never have given in to you of my own free will." . . . Goreu suddenly caught Ysbaddaden by the hair and dragged him to a mound and cut off his head. . . . And that night Culhwch slept with Olwen and she was his only wife as long as he lived.[45]

In their quests, Galahad and Culhwch had set out to find very different things. Galahad had sought a sacred object, the Grail, whereas Culhwch had determined to find the person he loved. Even though the goals were very different, the courage, enthusiasm, and dedication of the heroes were identical. Once they had set their goals, they had allowed nothing to stand in the way of accomplishing them. This "never give up" message was an inspiring lesson for many of the medieval Europeans who read or listened to these tales.

The Recovery of Thor's Hammer and Other Norse Quests

Chapter Five

The mythology of the Norse, including their stories of great quests and journeys, is filled with vigorous, colorful characters and events. However, there is also a bleak, pessimistic feeling pervading these tales, which perhaps derives in part from the unusual harshness of Norse life. These people, some of whom eventually came to be known as Vikings, lived in Europe's far northern reaches, inhabiting Scandinavia and later Iceland and other islands of the cold northern seas. (Scandinavia was settled in the second millennium B.C.; the Vikings crossed to Iceland about A.D. 840.) In these places they endured long, sometimes cruel winters; the growing seasons of their crops were short, so food was often scarce; and farmsteads and villages were commonly separated by a dozen or more miles, so many people had to learn to deal with isolation and loneliness. In

short, life was a constant struggle and therefore precarious.

The uncertainty of Norse life forced people to be tough, independent, capable of enduring hardship, and at times rough or even uncouth in bearing and manners. The gods and heroes they envisioned in their myths tend to be this way too. Take, for example, Thor, the god of thunder and the main character in one of the most famous Norse quests. As described by the noted scholar of the Norse, H. R. E. Davidson:

> In the myths, Thor appears as a burly, red-headed man, immensely strong, with a huge appetite, blazing eyes, and a beard, full of enormous vitality and power. He could increase his strength by wearing a special belt of might. Other prize possessions of his were his great

gloves, enabling him to grasp and shatter rocks, the chariot drawn by goats which took him across the sky, and his hammer. This last was regarded as the greatest of all the treasures of Asgard [the heavenly fortified citadel that constituted the home of the Norse gods], for Thor and his hammer formed a

The Norse god Odin, ruler of Asgard, sits on his throne.

protection against the giants and the monsters, the enemies of gods and men.[46]

It is the attempt to recover this fabulous hammer, after it has been stolen from Thor, that forms the nucleus of this great quest.

The other major Norse quests involve another prominent god—Odin. The ruler of Asgard, Odin was the oldest of the Norse gods and was attributed many roles, among them god of war, bringer of storms, master of magic, and deity of the underworld. Odin was able to maintain his vast power by two principal means. First, he was able to change his shape at will, which gave him a tremendous advantage over most of his enemies. Second, he possessed uncommon wisdom. And the search for the essential wisdom of the universe was the theme of one of his three famous quests.

Unfortunately, other Norse quests, along with many other exciting Norse myths, are undoubtedly lost forever. This is mainly because, as Davidson explains, "these stories have for the most part reached us in the work of Christian writers, and much of the original non-Christian tradition was edited, misunderstood, or forgotten before the myths reached us."[47] The main surviving Christian sources of the Norse myths include the *Poetic Edda* (or *Elder Edda*), an anonymous compilation of myths dating from about A.D. 1300 (a copy of which was discovered in an Icelandic farmhouse in the seventeenth century); the *Prose Edda* (or *Younger Edda*), a work by a thirteenth-century Icelandic chieftain, Snorri Sturluson; and a history of Denmark written in the twelfth century by a Dane named Saxo Grammaticus.[48]

The Missing Hammer

One of the poems of the *Elder Edda* tells the exciting, somewhat humorous, but at the same time brutal tale of the recovery of Thor's hammer. The story begins with the mighty Thor awakening one morning from a deep sleep. Reaching for his trusty hammer, the protector of Asgard, the god was dumbfounded to find that the precious object was nowhere to be found. Thor's confusion and surprise quickly changed to anger. The giants, his sworn enemies, were behind this theft, he bellowed. He could just feel it in his bones.

Wasting no time, Thor sought out Loki, the blood brother of Odin. Though part giant and a mischievous trickster, Loki sometimes dwelled in Asgard and helped the gods. On learning of the loss of the hammer, Loki observed that this was bad news indeed. Somehow, he said, they must retrieve the hammer before the giants living in various parts of the world heard of its theft. Otherwise, the giants would surely form a mighty army and attack Asgard. Thor agreed, and the two decided on a plan to recover the hammer. Loki would use his knowledge of the giants to find out where the object had been taken. But first he would ask the fertility goddess Freyja for assistance. According to Philip Wilkinson, Freyja,

The mighty god Thor, pictured here, awoke one morning to find his trusty hammer missing.

helped the crops grow, provided good catches for the fishermen, and came to the aid of women in childbirth. A goddess of magic and riches, she had a famous necklace . . . made by four dwarf brothers called the Brisings and a cloak of feathers called Valhamr.[49]

It was this cloak of feathers that Loki sought from Freyja, for it would allow him to fly swiftly to the land of the giants rather than having to travel by horse or other slower means (such as wagons or by foot). After hearing the news about the missing hammer, the goddess readily agreed to let Loki borrow the cloak. Take trusty Valhamr, she told him, and begin searching as swiftly as possible, for the safety of Asgard depended on it.

Donning Freyja's cloak, Loki bade Thor farewell and streaked away into the sky. Down from the lofty heights of Asgard he swooped and soared over the mountains and valleys of earth, where the race of humans dwelled. After several hours of frenzied flying, he saw below him the forbidding, desolate hills of Giantland. Cruising hither and

The Lay of Thrym

The myth of the theft and recovery of Thor's hammer comes from a section of the *Poetic Edda* called the Thrymskvitha, or the "Lay of Thrym." Like other parts of the Eddas, the original poem translates into English with difficulty and does not provide much in the way of detail and descriptive color. Thus, the modern myth-teller or reader must fill in the blanks, so to speak. Here are the opening four stanzas of the poem, as translated by Henry A. Bellows.

1
Wild was Thor when he awoke,
And when his mighty hammer he missed.
He shook his beard, his hair was bristling,
As the son of Jorth [i.e., Loki] about him [he] sought.
2
Hear now the speech that first he spake:
"Harken, Loki, and heed my words,
Nowhere on earth is it known to man,
Nor in heaven above: Our hammer is stolen."
3
To the dwelling fair of Freyja went they.
Hear now the speech that first he [Thor] spake:
"Wilt thou, Freyja, thy feather-dress lend me,
That so my hammer I may seek?"
4
"Thine it should be though of silver bright [said Freyja],
And I would give it [to you] though 'twere of gold."
Then Loki flew, and the feather-dress whirred,
Till he left behind him the home of the gods,
And reached at last the realm of the giants.

thither, Loki eventually caught sight of the king of the giants, Thrym, sitting on a rock. The huge, ugly being was humming a merry tune while he fashioned some leashes for his dogs, which, drooling and panting, surrounded the rock on which he sat.

Loki came in for a landing and told Thrym that he looked unusually happy for a giant. Looking up, Thrym greeted Loki with a wry smile and asked how things were going in Asgard. Loki was immediately suspicious of Thrym's polite manner, because he knew that the giant was in no way concerned about the well-being of the gods. As a matter of fact, Loki admitted, things were not going so well for the gods at that moment, for Thor's mighty hammer was missing. Did Thrym have some idea of the whereabouts of the lost artifact? Loki inquired. At first, Thrym gave Loki a cold stare. Then the giant burst into a fit of laughter so loud that the nearby hills shook and he admitted that he had stolen the hammer while Thor was sleeping. The gods would never find the hammer, Thrym said, because he had buried it in a secret place eight miles beneath the earth's surface. However, the giant said, Loki should tell poor, pathetic Thor not to despair too much. The "kindhearted" giant was willing to make the gods a deal: He would return the hammer in exchange for the beautiful goddess Freyja's hand in marriage.

Laughter in Asgard

Loki returned to Asgard as fast as he could and told Thor about his meeting with

The goddess Freyja, whose cloak of feathers Loki borrowed for his trip to the land of the giants.

Thrym and the deal that the king of the giants had offered. They then went to Freyja to inform her; predictably, she burst into a rage. Ripping off the necklace the dwarf brothers had made for her and throwing it against a wall, she swore she would never marry a giant. Instead, they should consult Odin and the other gods about what to do in this time of crisis.

In less than an hour, a great council of the gods gathered to consider the matter. All agreed that Freyja should never lower herself and marry a giant, and there was no doubt in anyone's mind that they must recover Thor's hammer as soon as possible. The question, said Odin, was how to go about retrieving the object, and he asked if anyone had any ideas for a workable plan. It was then that Odin's son, Heimdall, a guardian and trumpeter of Asgard, spoke up, saying that he had a plan in mind: Thor should go in quest of his hammer but do so disguised as Freyja, whom Thrym desired so much. Everyone laughed as the rugged, manly Thor objected strongly to the idea of dressing in women's clothes. But they convinced him that this was the only workable plan for regaining the lost hammer. And so, as described by modern myth-teller Dorothy Hosford,

> Most unwillingly, Thor let them dress him as a bride. They put a woman's dress upon him and hung keys at his girdle, as women wear them. They covered his face with a bridal veil and hung Freyja's necklace about his neck. They put a pretty cap upon his head. . . . [Loki also dressed as a woman, to impersonate Thor's serving maid.] Thor's chariot was brought and the goats were harnessed to it. Thor and Loki rode off, swift as the wind. Beneath the wheels of the chariot the mountains burst, earth burned with fire.[50]

The Marriage Celebration

The first leg of Thor's quest was a journey of many days to Giantland. When he and Loki, still in disguise, reached their destination, one of the giants saw them and alerted Thrym. The king of the giants was greatly excited, since he believed that the gods had accepted his deal and sent the lovely Freyja to be his bride. He ordered that a lavish wedding feast and celebration be arranged as quickly as possible.

That very evening, Thrym welcomed a large company of giants to his banquet hall in a cave hollowed out of the inside of a mountain. There was music and vast quantities of food and wine, all in honor of the king's marriage to the goddess Freyja. Thor, still fuming over having to wear a dress and veil, sat with Loki near Thrym at the head of the largest table. When the food was served, Thor consumed an entire ox and several large salmon, not to mention the load of sweets that had been prepared for the king's bride. Thrym exclaimed aloud that in all his days he had never seen a woman eat so much and wanted to know how this could be happening. Luckily for the gods, the clever Loki was quick with an answer. He told Thrym that Freyja had been so thrilled by the idea of becoming the giant's wife that she had been unable to eat for nine days. Now that she was with Thrym at last, her appetite had come back and she was making up for lost time.

Thrym was apparently satisfied with this explanation. But when the giant noticed two red eyes burning fiercely from beneath

Wielding his formidable hammer, Thor dashes across the countryside.

the veil, he shrank back in apprehension. What about her eyes? he inquired of Loki. Why did they burn so hotly, almost like the coals of a fire? Thinking quickly again, Loki replied that during those same nine days and nights, Freyja also did not sleep, so her eyes were terribly bloodshot.

Again, the somewhat dim-witted giant was satisfied with Loki's explanation. It was soon time for the wedding ceremony to begin, so at the king's order, a servant brought in Thor's hammer. Following the custom of the groom presenting the bride his most prized possession as a wedding gift, Thrym placed the hammer on Thor's lap. Now, Thrym declared, the lovely Freyja would be his forever.

But then a gruff voice from beneath the veil told Thrym that he should not count on having a happy life with Freyja. A look of confusion shrouded Thrym's face and the hall went completely silent. Suddenly, Thor yanked the veil from his face, revealing his true identity to the startled giants. Calling the giant king a thief, the god raised the monstrous, lethal hammer high above the terrified Thrym and swung it downward, crushing the giant's skull. As the king's lifeless body collapsed in a heap, the other giants hurried around in confusion in an attempt to escape. But Thor kept on swinging the hammer, smashing and killing them all. Finally, Thor and Loki, both still clad in dresses, were the only living beings left standing in the blood-soaked chamber.

Loki was to listen well, Thor said as they removed and discarded their women's clothes. From that day forward, no one was to mention what Thor was wearing when he regained his hammer. And he would tolerate no further laughter at his expense. Loki knew that Thor meant business and with a smile agreed to the demands. But ever after, Loki secretly hated the god of thunder and waited patiently for the day he might see him fall from power.

The High Price of Wisdom

The difference between the goals of Thor's quest and those of Odin's quests speaks volumes about the differences between the personalities and interests of these two gods. Because battle and killing were a way of life with Thor, he wanted to retrieve a mighty weapon that could be used to crush his and

Asgard's enemies. By contrast, the things that Odin sought—wisdom, the secrets of magic, and the gift of poetry—were concerned with thinking, knowing, and creating. So they were more intangible and also more difficult to acquire because they involved certain sacrifices on the part of the seeker. Odin was willing to make these sacrifices because above all else he desired to develop the powers of his mind.

In his first quest, for example, Odin found that to attain his goal he had to give up one of the most precious physical attributes possessed by gods and humans. One morning, as he did nearly every day, he sat on his throne in Asgard's great hall. His majestic ravens, two huge birds named Thought and Memory, perched on his shoulders. At his feet sat two wolves. Because Odin valued knowledge above all else, he sent Thought and Memory out to watch and listen to all that was happening in the world. In the evening, as they did nearly every evening, the ravens returned, and they whispered into the god's ear what they had seen and heard.

But this time Odin was not satisfied. He wanted more than simple facts, he told his ravens. He wanted to acquire true wisdom of the ways of the world and of divine and human nature. The leader of the gods knew that Asgard, the earth's surface, and other parts of the known universe were all supported by a vast tree known as Yggdrasil. Odin had heard from reliable sources that deep inside the roots of Yggdrasil, at a place where the sky and ocean met, there existed

The World of the Norse Myths

In this excerpt from her informative volume *Gods and Myths of Northern Europe*, the late Hilda R. E. Davidson, a world-renowned expert on Norse mythology, gives this general description of the world and some of the fabulous beings of that mythology.

This world had for its center a great tree, a mighty ash called Yggdrasil. So huge was this tree that its branches stretched out over heaven and earth alike. Three roots supported the great trunk, and one passed into the realm of the Aesir [the Norse gods], a second into that of the frost-giants, and a third into the realm of the dead. Beneath the root in giant-land was the spring of Mimer, whose waters contained wisdom and understanding. Odin had given one of his eyes for the right to drink a single draft of that precious water. Below the tree in the kingdom of the Aesir was the sacred spring of fate, the Well of Urd. Here every day the gods assembled for their court of law, to settle disputes, and discuss common problems. All came on horseback except Thor, who preferred to wade through the rivers that lay in his path, and they were led by Odin on the finest of all steeds, the eight-legged horse Sleipnir. The gods galloped over the bridge Bifrost, a rainbow bridge that glowed with fire. They alone might cross it, and the giants, who longed to do so, were held back. Near the spring of fate dwelled three maidens called the Norns, who ruled the destinies of men. . . . At the root of the tree lay a great serpent, with many scores of lesser snakes, and these gnawed continually at Yggdrasil.

The gigantic world tree the Norse called Yggdrasil.

a special well, and sipping from its waters would supposedly bring the drinker great wisdom. Odin had also heard that the well of wisdom was guarded by a giant named Mimer, who was very wise because each morning he took a drink from the well.

Odin thought it was unfair that Mimer, a giant (and therefore a member of a race the gods disliked), was able to acquire more

The Norse god Odin travels through the land of the humans on one of his quests.

wisdom than the leader of the gods. So Odin decided to seek out Mimer and the well and gain for himself the wisdom he longed to possess. Putting on his traveling cloak and hat and grasping his stout staff, he set out the next morning. His long journey took him down across the bridge that connected Asgard to the earth, past the land where humans dwelled, and into the roots of mighty Yggdrasil. Odin searched high and low and asked directions from all he met along the way.

Finally, the god found the secret grotto where Mimer guarded the well of wisdom. Odin called out to a huge form that lay sleeping on a bed of Yggdrasil's giant leaves and said that he must be addressing Mimer, guardian of the well. Yawning and stretching, the giant rather groggily replied that he must be speaking to Odin, leader of the gods. When the surprised Odin asked how Mimer knew his identity, since they had never met before, the giant explained that drinking from the well had made him very wise, and in his wisdom he could foresee that the greatest of the gods would one day come seeking wisdom for himself.

Odin wasted no time getting to the point. Since he had traveled so far to acquire wisdom, he said, he trusted that Mimer would readily allow him to drink from the well. Mimer smiled and stood up, his great bulk towering to more than fifty times Odin's height. First, said the giant, anyone who drank from the well had to make a personal sacrifice. He or she must pay a very dear price, for true wisdom did not come cheap. Odin boldly insisted that Mimer name this price, for whatever it was, he would gladly pay it. The giant then informed the god that the price was one of his eyes. Since gaining wisdom would allow Odin to see things his eyes could not, he believed he could afford to part with one of them. Though reluctant to do so, Odin agreed to the exchange. That day he eagerly drank from the well of wisdom and gained many new insights into the secrets of life. And as modern myth-teller Abbie F. Brown tells it,

> When Odin went away from the grotto, he left at the bottom of the dark pool one of his fiery eyes, which twinkled and winked up through the magic depths like the reflection of a star. This is how Odin lost his eye, and why from that day he was careful to pull his gray hat low over his face when he wanted to pass unnoticed. For by this oddity folk could easily recognize the wise lord of Asgard.[51]

Odin's Other Quests

Odin, though happy that he had acquired more wisdom than anyone (except for Mimer himself), was still not satisfied. Beyond mere wisdom, he told Thought and Memory one day, there was magic. Odin desired to know the secrets of the runes, the mysterious written symbols that held magical powers over the forces of nature. Now that he was a very wise being, Odin knew that finding the secret of the runes would not be easy, and it would require a great personal sacrifice. Moreover, the quest for the secrets of magic would not involve a journey to some faraway place but, rather, a pilgrimage into the self. Odin would have to search inside his own mind, body, and soul to discover whether he possessed the courage, endurance, and insight required to achieve the knowledge he sought.

In his wisdom, Odin also realized that this inner quest would have to be accompanied by great suffering, for there was no other way to test his mental and physical resolve. He went to one of the branches of Yggdrasil, the tree of life, and hung himself from it. Then he plunged his spear into his side and left it there, allowing the blood to seep out of his body and down the weapon's shaft. For nine days and nine nights, the leader of the gods hung there in agony, alone and without food or drink. Finally, on the morning of the tenth day, he gazed down into the world of the dead, and there he saw the outlines of several magical runes materialize before him. Suddenly, he possessed the powers of healing the sick, speaking to the dead, and seeing into the future.

Odin's third and last quest was for the gift of poetry. Even though he appreciated

Odin rides his horse Sleipnir as his faithful wolves and birds follow along.

having the powers of wisdom and magic, these seemed hollow without creativity. He believed that the ability to move the gods and humans through beautiful, inspiring words was just as important a power for a leader to have. Odin learned that a special liquid called the Mead of Poetry turned whoever drank it into an accomplished poet. The mead was stored in a large keg in a cave in Giantland and guarded by the daughter of a giant named Suttung, but Odin was not intimidated in the least. He journeyed to Giantland and cut a tunnel through the side of the mountain in which the cave was hidden. Then he turned himself into a snake and slithered through the tunnel until he reached the cave and the keg of mead. After drinking his fill, Odin slithered back out, transformed himself into an eagle, and flew home to Asgard. In time, the wise and generous Odin came to share the secrets of wisdom, the runes, and poetry with ordinary men and women. These precious things, the fruits of his quests, became known as Odin's gifts to humanity.

The quests of Thor and Odin had one thing in common. They all involved finding objects or qualities that gave those who possessed them great or unusual powers. Perhaps this fascination with superhuman powers reflected the more mundane realities of Norse life. In the constant and difficult fight for survival in the sometimes harsh wilderness of northern Europe, the average person may have felt powerless and taken a little comfort in tales of valiant men and gods who had managed to break free from such limitations.

The Vision Quest and Other Journeys of the Plains Indians

The mythologies of the Native Americans, often referred to as American Indians, had no large-scale, highly organized quests comparable to Jason and the Golden Fleece, Aeneas and the Roman foundation, or the quest for the Holy Grail. Native American epic journeys tend instead to be less organized and more informal, often in the form of tribal migrations. Most of the real migrations on which these myths are based occurred well before the appearance of whites in North America. However, some happened after—and indeed as a result of—white settlement. The Cheyenne, for example, did not always inhabit the midwestern plains, their homeland during the early years of the United States. The tribe, along with other Plains tribes, apparently migrated from the east, probably from the region of the Great Lakes, in prior cen-

turies. As explained here by scholar Carl Waldman,

The Great Plains culture area is unique in the sense that the typical Indian subsistence pattern and related lifeways evolved long after [white] contact. It was the advent of horses, brought to North America by whites . . . that made the new life on the plains possible. With increased mobility and prowess, former village and farming tribes of the river valleys became nomadic hunters, especially of the buffalo. And other tribes migrated onto the plains from elsewhere to partake of this life-style. With time, varying tribal customs blended into what is sometimes referred to as the Composite Plains Tribe, shaped by the horse and buffalo culture.[52]

One of the most distinctive myths of this Plains buffalo culture is the story of the Cheyenne wanderings in search of a habitable land.

Another kind of journey prevalent in the mythologies of a number of Native American tribes is that in which a creator being roams the earth, planting the seeds of civilization here and there. Among the most famous of these creators was Lone Man. Variations of his story were told by many different tribes, particularly those of the plains.

A different kind of mythological journey that was popular among the Plains Indians was an inward rather than outward one. This was known as the vision quest. In some ways, the vision quest resembled the Norse god Odin's quest for the secrets of the magic runes; both involved a character exploring his or her inner being. There were also powerful spiritual and dream elements in the vision quest, as noted expert on Native American myths, the late Cottie Burland explained:

The religious beliefs of the plains Indians centered on an ill-defined, but omnipresent [existing in all

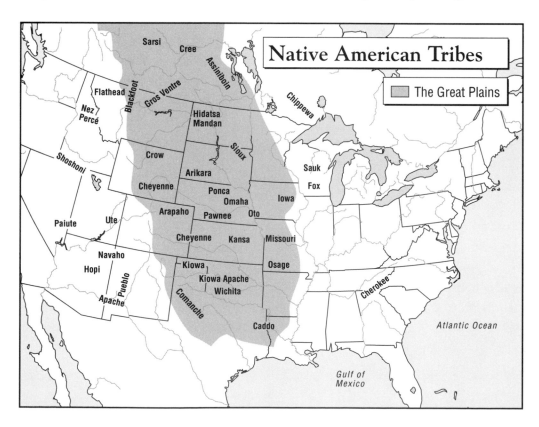

Native American Tribes

The Great Plains

places and times] supernatural power which manifested itself all around them—in the sun, moon, and stars, in animals and birds, and in natural forces such as wind, thunder, and rain. Some tribes developed sophisticated philosophies concerning the roles of these beings in the universe, but for others they remained mysterious forces which controlled the natural world, but which could be persuaded, through prayers and offerings, to use their powers for the benefit of human beings. Powerful beings communicated with people through dreams and visions and thus the individual vision

The Diversity of Native American Culture and Myths

No single, universal set of myths exists for the American Indians as a whole. This is because the Native American peoples did not belong to a single cultural group with one widely accepted pantheon of gods and other mythical characters, as did the Greeks, Romans, and Norse. Before and long after the appearance of Europeans in North America, the Native American peoples of the continent belonged to many separate groups and tribes that displayed a large, impressive, and rich cultural and religious diversity.

This diversity was based on various factors. The most important was the wide variation of geographic and physical settings in which these peoples lived, ranging from the freezing, treeless wastelands of northern Canada, to the more temperate, heavily forested lands of what is now the eastern United States, to the rolling plains of the Midwest on which roamed vast herds of buffalo, and to the hot, dry deserts of the Southwest, where the people often constructed their homes from sun-baked mud.

The upshot of this wide variety of settings was that separate tribes or regional groups of tribes developed their own distinctive religious views, gods, and myths. The nature of the heroes and events of these myths was heavily colored by their local settings. The Inuit living near the Bering Sea (in northern Canada), for instance, believed that one of the major predators of that region, the killer whale, could transform itself into a wolf. In that form it supposedly roamed the icy tundra looking for people to eat. The myths of the Cheyenne, who lived on the Great Plains, were often very different. Their lives revolved around the hunting of buffalo, and one of their heroes, Falling Star, was famous for killing a white crow that flew ahead of human hunters and warned the buffalo to flee.

quest was an important way of gaining spiritual power. To this end, young men (and sometimes women) would go alone to some desolate place to fast and pray for guidance from the spirits. As a result of their deprivations, they quite often did have visions in which spirits appeared to aid them and to instruct them in the sacred rituals necessary for their success in life.[53]

The Rules of the Quest

Such vision quests were obviously private affairs, and usually the details of these experiences were revealed only to relatives and close friends. However, all vision quests involved certain basic, repeated practices and other elements—in a sense, rules—which varied somewhat from tribe to tribe. In order to experience the desired visions and ultimately to communicate with a spirit or spirits, the seeker was expected to follow the rules. When he or she failed to do so, there were negative consequences.

One such failed vision quest is the subject of a story told by the Shoshoni, a Plains tribe that lived in what is now eastern Wyoming. One night, a young warrior named Taivotsi (meaning "little white man") had a dream in which he heard a voice. The voice commanded him to go to Willow Creek and camp near the ancient drawings on the rock walls. If he followed the rules of the vision quest, he would be

An etching shows an Indian warrior praying. Native Americans were, and remain, a very spiritual people.

visited by a powerful spirit who would reward him with good hunting and the beneficial gifts that come of it.

When Taivotsi woke up, he was excited at the prospect of a vision quest and of communing with the spirits. That very day, he rode his horse northward into the hills for several hours until he saw the rocks of Willow Creek looming in the distance. The

Willow Creek, located in Wyoming, is where the warrior Taivotsi went to commune with the spirits. He was unsuccessful in his first attempt.

ancient rock carvings there were considered sacred gifts of the spirits and constituted the main focus of Shoshoni worship. Nearly every Shoshoni embarking on a vision quest went to Willow Creek, and Taivotsi was no exception.

Once he reached the sacred area, the young man carefully followed the rules laid down by tradition. He tethered his horse about two hundred yards from the rock drawings. Then he went to the nearest stream, stripped off his clothes, and took a bath, a ritual intended to cleanse him not only physically but also mentally. Next, Taivotsi walked, still naked, to a place beside the rock drawings and made camp.

Finally, he spread a blanket and laid down flat on it, facing up at the sky.

A Test of Resolve

Taivotsi relaxed and prayed and then laid very still, hoping to have a vision. An hour passed, then two, and then three, and eventually the sun went down and he could see the stars appear up above, twinkling like tiny distant flames on the black dome of the night. Suddenly, an owl swooped down, seemingly from nowhere, and pecked at the young man's chest. Taivotsi knew he should not move, for he had been told that animals often visited a person on a quest and did things to test his or her resolve. The owl pecked at him several more times, but when he did not respond, the bird disappeared. Next, a bear arrived and pushed Taivotsi around with its huge paw. Once again, the young man managed to resist and control his fear, so the bear too disappeared. A deer and a coyote also visited the naked man, who did not flinch, even when the coyote bit him on the leg.

Finally, however, Taivotsi received a visitor that he could not deal with. The visitor was a snake, and because Taivotsi was terrified of snakes he cried out, jumped up, and ran away. Needless to say, his attempt to achieve a visionary dream state and commune with the spirit had failed. But what

was worse was that he had been so close to his goal—the snake that had scared him away was the form taken by the very spirit he had sought. The spirit was insulted that the man had summoned it and then abandoned it, so it punished Taivotsi by making his legs lame and forcing him to walk on crutches.

The following year, Taivotsi tried once more to commune with the spirit. And again the man broke one of the rules that governed the quest. This time, the spirit struck Taivotsi's eyes, leaving him almost blind. Afterward, as the failed seeker began hobbling home on his crutches, he repeatedly fell down in the dirt because he could

A snake like this one frightened Taivotsi. What he did not know was that the snake was actually the spirit he sought to contact.

barely see the rocks and other obstacles in his path.

Moved by this pathetic sight, the spirit had a change of heart and made itself visible to the man. Taivotsi should listen carefully, it said. The man had broken the rules of the quest and that is why he had been punished. However, it seemed to the spirit that the man's heart was in the right place, and now Taivotsi was so pitiful that it would be wrong to let him suffer any more. The spirit told the man to go to Willow Creek on the following day and there he would find a large deer to hunt for food, hides, and antlers.

The next morning, Taivotsi woke up to find his legs and eyes restored to normal. He went to Willow Creek, as instructed, and found the deer, which he killed and butchered. And thereafter, he was successful in (and profited from) his quests to commune with the spirit.

The Long Wanderings of the Cheyenne

Another, more powerful spirit, known as the Great Medicine, brought good hunting to

A Myth Based on Real Events

The Cheyenne myth of the tribe's great journey from a forested area near a large lake to the open spaces of the Great Plains is actually supported by archaeological evidence, as explained in this excerpt from an article (published in the *Encyclopedia of North American Indians*) by modern Cheyenne historian Rubie Sootkis.

Oral tradition tells of a time when the people who called themselves Tsetschestahase, and are now called by others "Cheyenne". . . were fishermen, living in a marshy area by a large body of water, living probably very much like their more easterly Algonquian relatives. Next, they were villagers who lived in earth lodges, planted corn, and hunted without horses. Later, after migrating westward onto the Great Plains, they received from the Sacred Mountain (modern Bear Butte, South Dakota) the buffalo and developed the lifeway for which they are best known today: the classic horse-buffalo-tipi complex of the high plains. Archaeology confirms the transition from semi-sedentary earth-lodge villages to high-plains life, and the re-invention of Cheyenne culture in the new environment. This transformation . . . probably took place in the mid–seventeenth century . . . . The famous Cheyenne Council of Forty-four also developed during the classic high-plains period. Its fame derives from the fact that, unlike many other Native American governments, the council was a vaguely representative body with conventional rules of procedure that non-Indian people could comprehend.

the Shoshoni's neighbors, the Cheyenne. In fact, one of the Cheyenne's most important myths told how the Great Medicine spirit fashioned an earthly paradise where forests grew thick with shade trees, game was always plentiful, and the climate was always pleasant. According to the legend, the Cheyenne lived in this beneficial land for many generations, along with a race of people who were covered from head to foot with long hair. Both the Cheyenne and the hairy people were able to communicate with animals, which made them very close to nature.

Eventually, the hairy people left the area and migrated toward the southwest. In time, for reasons that no one knows, the Cheyenne decided to follow the hairy people. The Indians packed up their belongings and headed southwestward, away from their familiar forests and onto a series of vast, rolling plains. They found the hairy people living in caves and tried to greet them, but for some reason the hairy people were now afraid of the Indians and shied away from them. Eventually, all the hairy people either died or disappeared, leaving the Cheyenne alone on the plains.

All went well for the Cheyenne for several years. But then one day some members of the tribe had visions in which they heard a spirit warn them of impending doom. Soon, the spirit said, a great flood would come upon the land and all living things would die. Therefore, the people must flee. Doing as the spirit advised, the Cheyenne returned to their original homeland. It was a long, difficult, and exhausting journey, yet they were happy to be returning to the beneficial land of their ancestors. To their dismay, however, the Cheyenne found that the land was no longer a paradise, and most of the once-plentiful game had vanished. What is more, they could no longer talk with the few animals that remained.

One Cheyenne chief declared that his people would be better off on the plains, where there were many buffalo to feed and clothe them. Eventually, he said, the floodwaters would subside, leaving the plains livable again. Everyone else agreed with him. So, once more the people made the long trek overland to the plains, where, sure enough, the floodwaters had subsided, leaving the land green and fruitful. There, the Cheyenne dwelled for many more generations. And in the fullness of time, other Indians migrated there to enjoy its benefits, so the people once again had neighbors.

Walking on the Waters

Another similar transformation involving the creation of habitable land from what had been floodwaters occurs in the Mandan tale of the journey of Lone Man. (The Mandan were a tribe that lived along the Missouri River in what is now North Dakota.) Indeed, Lone Man's great trek, as the Mandan tribal elders told it, began so long ago that the face of the earth was still covered with water and there were no people at all. Lone Man was walking on the surface of the waters when he met another person, who called himself First Man. After they introduced themselves, First Man

When Lone Man encountered a Mandan village like this one, he saw how the villagers struggled to survive and endeavored to help them.

asked Lone Man where he had come from and who his parents were. Lone Man was perplexed and tried hard to remember. But he could not. He said that in truth he did not know exactly where he had come from. All he knew was that he was there. First Man smiled and explained that it was the same with him. Since they somehow did exist, First Man said, it made sense for them to create a more hospitable environment, one in which they could make homes for themselves. For that, they would need to make land in the midst of all this water.

Lone Man agreed with this idea. The two continued to walk along the water's surface until they spied a duck paddling along. They instructed the duck to dive down to the bottom of the ocean and bring up some earth, and the duck did so. It repeated this

process three more times, so there were four pieces of earth, which Lone Man and First Man now used to create land, and from which the first grass and trees began to grow. Before long, there were mountains, plains, valleys, streams, and ponds. Next, Lone Man and his companion fashioned buffalo, deer, cattle, sheep, and other animals to populate the land.

Several years passed. And then the two superhuman beings stumbled on a pleasant surprise. They found human tribes living on the land and attempting to eke out a living by hunting, fishing, and growing corn. First Man and Lone Man had no more an idea of where the humans had come from than where they themselves had come from. Fascinated, Lone Man began to observe one of these tribes, the Mandan, while First Man said good-bye and journeyed on toward the west.

After watching the Mandan for several seasons, Lone Man saw that sometimes, no matter how hard they struggled, they suffered from hunger and other deprivations. Because his heart was equivalent to his physical strength (which was considerable), he took pity on them. He wanted to share in their struggle and to make their lives easier by showing them better ways of doing some things. And the best way to do this, he decided, was to become a human.

There are different versions of how Lone Man accomplished this crucial transformation. One version says that he shrank himself down and entered a kernel of corn, and when a young woman ate the kernel she became pregnant and gave birth to Lone Man in human form. Another version of the story claims that Lone Man took the form of a dead buffalo floating in a stream. A young girl came along and ate some of the buffalo meat, which caused her to become pregnant and give birth to Lone Man.

Lone Man grew into a remarkably handsome and popular young man. He showed the people how to make warmer and more beautiful clothes. He also demonstrated new and more effective ways of finding and trapping animals, so the people had more to eat and famine became

rare. In addition, Lone Man became a peacemaker. Whenever members of the tribe quarreled with one another or with people of neighboring tribes, he stepped in and mediated, showing that war and violence could sometimes be avoided by using common sense and compassion.

Eventually, Lone Man faced his greatest test. A powerful and malicious being named

A modern Mandan woman in traditional garb. According to a Mandan myth, Lone Man saved the tribe from a great flood.

Maninga attempted to destroy Lone Man and his people by transforming itself into a great flood. As Burland tells it,

> At this time there were five Mandan villages full of people, and as the flood came higher the villages were abandoned one by one. Lone Man led his people to the last village. There he planted a sacred cedar tree. . . . Then he built a small stockade of willow planks. It was called the Great Canoe, though it never floated. As the flood grew, it lapped the sides of the Great Canoe.[54]

Luckily, Lone Man proved stronger and smarter than Maninga and forced the evil being into making the waters recede. After this defeat, Maninga never bothered the Mandan again.

A few years after this incident, Lone Man felt that his work was done and that it was time for him to move on. He had taught the Mandan better ways to hunt and how to make peace and had saved them from destruction, and he could not think of anything else he could do for them. Anyway, he had begun his life as a wanderer, and the urge to travel became strong in him again. One day he packed his things and said farewell to the Mandan, who were sad to see him go. Then he departed and disappeared over the western horizon. According to Burland, "Some of the stockade that the Indians believed to be the remains of the Great Canoe can still be seen at the old Mandan village on the left bank of the Upper Missouri."[55]

Reaching for the Horizon

The diverse nature of these Native American tales of quests and journeys, as well as those of other ancient peoples, illustrate that such treks had a wide range of goals and outcomes. Some, like the stories of the Cheyenne, Odysseus, and Aeneas, dealt with the search for a homeland. Others, including those of the Shoshoni warrior Taivotsi and the Norse god Odin, described the attempt of a hero to explore his inner being. Still others were searches for fabulous, valuable, or powerful objects.

From the midst of this colorful array of diversity emerges a common thread—the desire of human beings to strive for something out of the ordinary, to achieve, experience, or benefit from the *extra*ordinary. The goal always seems to loom just beyond the horizon in some strange, mysterious, wonderful, or terrible place. But mythical, larger-than-life figures like Gilgamesh, Jason, Galahad, Odin, and Lone Man will always drive themselves to reach that horizon, for they serve as the outward expression of the burning spirit of curiosity and adventure that exists deep within all people in all times and places.

Notes

Introduction: Epic Searchers, Old and New

1. Apollonius of Rhodes, *Argonautica*, published as *The Voyage of the Argo*. Trans. E. V. Rieu. New York: Penguin Books, 1971, pp. 50–51.
2. Philip Wilkinson, *The Illustrated Dictionary of Mythology*. New York: Dorling Kindersley, 1998, p. 12.

Chapter 1: Gilgamesh and the Search for Immortality

3. John Gray, *Near Eastern Mythology*. New York: Peter Bedrick Books, 1982, p. 40.
4. Quoted in Stephanie Dalley, trans., *Myths from Mesopotamia*. New York: Oxford University Press, 1989, pp. 52–53.
5. Norma L. Goodrich, *Ancient Myths*. New York: New American Library, 1960, p. 14.
6. Quoted in Dalley, *Myths from Mesopotamia*, pp. 71–72.
7. Quoted in Dalley, *Myths from Mesopotamia*, pp. 92–93.
8. Goodrich, *Ancient Myths*, p. 21.
9. Quoted in Dalley, *Myths from Mesopotamia*, p. 18.
10. Quoted in Dalley, *Myths from Mesopotamia*, p. 112.
11. Quoted in Dalley, *Myths from Mesopotamia*, pp. 113–14.

Chapter 2: Two Greek Epic Journeys: The Adventures of Jason and Odysseus

12. Other ancient writers described episodes in Jason's life that took place after the recovery of the Golden Fleece. For instance, the famous Greek playwright Euripides' great tragedy *Medea* deals with the grisly revenge exacted by the title character, who had helped Jason obtain the fleece, after he rejects her for another woman.
13. Edith Hamilton, *Mythology*. New York: New American Library, 1940, p. 17.
14. Valerius Flaccus, *Argonautica*, quoted in Rhoda A. Hendricks, trans., *Classical Gods and Heroes: Myths as Told by the Ancient Authors*. New York: Morrow Quill, 1974, p. 183.
15. Apollonius, *Argonautica*, p. 38.
16. Apollonius, *Argonautica*, pp. 44–45.
17. Charles Kingsley, *The Heroes*. Santa Rosa, CA: Classics Press, 1968, pp. 73–74.
18. The Greek word *harpyai* means "snatchers," and the Harpies were originally pictured (in Homer, for example) as snatching people's souls. Later, they earned a reputation for harassing people and fouling their food.
19. Apollonius, *Argonautica*, p. 80.
20. Apollonius, *Argonautica*, pp. 126–27.
21. Homer, *Odyssey*. Trans. E. V. Rieu. Baltimore: Penguin Books, 1961, p. 141.
22. Homer, *Odyssey*, p. 142.
23. Homer, *Odyssey*, pp.149–50.
24. Homer, *Odyssey*, p. 172.
25. Homer, *Odyssey*, p. 330.

Chapter 3: The Journey of Aeneas, Father of the Roman Race

26. Sallust, *Conspiracy of Catiline*, in *Sallust: The Jugurthine War/The Conspiracy of Catiline*. Trans. S. A. Handford. New York: Penguin Books, 1988, p. 220. Sallust attributed this speech to the famous politician-soldier, Julius Caesar, although the

wording is more likely the historian's own.

27. T. J. Cornell, *The Beginnings of Rome: Italy and Rome from the Bronze Age to the Punic Wars (c. 1000–264 B.C.).* London: Routledge, 1995, p. 65.

28. Virgil, *Aeneid.* Trans. Patric Dickinson. New York: New American Library, 1961, p. 9.

29. Virgil, *Aeneid*, p. 75.

30. Goodrich, *Ancient Myths*, pp. 210–11.

31. Virgil, *Aeneid*, pp. 57–58.

32. Virgil, *Aeneid*, p. 72.

33. Virgil, *Aeneid*, p. 82.

34. Virgil, *Aeneid*, pp. 83–85.

35. Virgil, *Aeneid*, pp. 132–33.

36. Virgil, *Aeneid*, pp. 141–42.

37. Goodrich, *Ancient Myths*, pp. 249–50.

38. Virgil, *Aeneid*, p. 14.

Chapter 4: Celtic Quests: The Search for Love and Perfect Morality

39. As Europeans, the Celts naturally came into frequent contact with the Greeks and Romans, who inhabited and controlled southern Europe. (The Greeks called them *Keltoi*, the Romans *Celtae*.) Because the Celts had no cities, preferring a pastoral existence characterized by simple farms and villages, the Greco-Roman world viewed them as barbarians. In reality, even though they were less advanced materially speaking than the Greeks and Romans, the Celts were no less civilized; they had laws, considerable social organization, and rich, well-developed religious traditions.

40. Wilkinson, *The Illustrated Dictionary of Mythology*, p. 92.

41. P. M. Matarasso, trans., *The Quest of the Holy Grail.* New York: Penguin Books, 1969, pp. 43–44.

42. *The Quest of the Holy Grail*, pp. 42–43.

43. *The Quest of the Holy Grail*, p. 283.

44. Quoted in Richard Barber, ed., *The Arthurian Legends: An Illustrated Anthology.* New York: Peter Bedrick Books, 1979, p. 36.

45. Quoted in Barber, *The Arthurian Legends*, p. 43.

Chapter 5: The Recovery of Thor's Hammer and Other Norse Quests

46. H. R. Ellis Davidson, *Scandinavian Mythology.* New York: Peter Bedrick Books, 1986, pp. 59–60.

47. Davidson, *Scandinavian Mythology*, p. 9.

48. Saxo's history is also the original source of the story of a Danish prince and his family troubles, which William Shakespeare later adapted for his play *Hamlet.*

49. Wilkinson, *The Illustrated Dictionary of Mythology*, p. 83.

50. Dorothy Hosford, *Thunder of the Gods.* New York: Holt, Rinehart, and Winston, 1952, p. 60.

51. Abbie F. Brown, *In the Days of the Giants.* Boston: Houghton Mifflin, 1906, p. 17.

Chapter 6: The Vision Quest and Other Journeys of the Plains Indians

52. Carl Waldman, *Atlas of the North American Indian.* New York: Facts On File, 1985, p. 40.

53. Cottie Burland, *North American Indian Mythology.* Rev. Marion Wood. New York: Peter Bedrick Books, 1985, pp. 76–77.

54. Burland, *North American Indian Mythology*, p. 84.

55. Burland, *North American Indian Mythology*, p. 84.

For Further Reading

David Bellingham, *An Introduction to Greek Mythology*. Secaucus, NJ: Chartwell Books, 1989. Explains the major Greek myths and legends and their importance to the ancient Greeks; contains many beautiful photos and drawings.

Peter Connolly, *The Legend of Odysseus*. New York: Oxford University Press, 1986. An excellent, easy-to-read summary of the events of Homer's *Iliad* and *Odyssey*, including many informative sidebars about the way people lived in Mycenaean times; also contains many stunning illustrations re-creating the fortresses, homes, ships, and armor of the period.

Arthur Cotterell, *Celtic Mythology*. New York: Lorenz Books, 1998. This first-rate introductory mythology book features an encyclopedia-style, alphabetical listing of mythical characters, supported by many beautiful color illustrations; highly recommended.

Richard Erdoes and Alfonso Ortiz, eds., *American Indian Myths and Legends*. New York: Pantheon Books, 1985. Dozens of entertaining Native American tales are included in this well-written volume.

Dorothy Hosford, *Thunder of the Gods*. New York: Holt, Rinehart, and Winston, 1952. A highly entertaining telling of several of the most famous Norse myths, including the theft of and quest for Thor's hammer.

Charles Kingsley, *The Heroes*. Santa Rosa, CA: Classics Press, 1968. This is a reprint of the original book by Kingsley, the renowned nineteenth-century social reformer, university professor, and classical scholar, a work he wrote for his three children; contains his superb retellings of the stories of Jason, Perseus, Theseus, and Heracles.

Don Nardo, ed., *Readings on Homer*. San Diego: Greenhaven Press, 1998. This useful volume contains several somewhat scholarly yet readable essays about various aspects of the *Iliad* and *Odyssey*, as well as about Homer's style and impact, each essay by a noted expert in the classics.

Mary P. Osborne, *Favorite Norse Myths*. New York: Scholastic, 1996. A handsomely illustrated compilation of Norse myths, including stories involving monsters, giants, dwarves, and Odin's quests.

Neil Philip, *The Illustrated Book of Myths: Tales and Legends of the World*. New York: Dorling Kindersley, 1995. An excellent introduction to world mythology for young people, enlivened with many stunning photos and drawings.

———, *Mythology*. New York: Knopf, 1999. Another fine beginners' mythology volume by Philip, who has written a number of other children's books on the subject, including *Fairy Tales of Eastern Europe* and *The Arabian Nights*.

Major Works Consulted

Thomas Bulfinch, *Bulfinch's Mythology*. New York: Dell, 1959. This is one of several versions of this well-known and useful work, which is itself a modern compilation of two of Bulfinch's original books— *The Age of Fable* (1855), a retelling of the Greek and Roman myths, and *The Age of Chivalry* (1858), an account of the Arthurian legends.

Cottie Burland, *North American Indian Mythology*. Rev. Marion Wood. New York: Peter Bedrick Books, 1985. This volume, by the late Cottie Burland, a scholar at the British Museum and an authority on Native American myths, is divided according to geographic regions, such as "Hunters of the Northern Forests," "Farmers of the Eastern Woodlands," and "Dwellers on the Mesas."

Proinsias Mac Cana, *Celtic Mythology*. New York: Peter Bedrick Books, 1985. A well-organized and informative description of Celtic folklore, including some of the tales of Arthur and the other traditional heroes of yore.

H. R. Ellis Davidson, *Gods and Myths of Northern Europe*. Baltimore: Penguin Books, 1964. This is one of the best general overviews of Norse mythology, written by one of the acknowledged experts in the field.

———, *Scandinavian Mythology*. New York: Peter Bedrick Books, 1986. Another excellent overview of Norse myths, this one beautifully illustrated with many photos of Scandinavian vistas and Norse artifacts.

Michael Grant, *Myths of the Greeks and Romans*. New York: New American Library, 1962. One of the twentieth century's most prolific and respected classical historians here delivers a fine rendition of the important Greek and Roman myths, along with plenty of background information and analysis.

John Gray, *Near Eastern Mythology*. New York: Peter Bedrick Books, 1982. This synopsis of the major myths of the Mesopotamians and other ancient Near Eastern peoples is well written and authoritative.

Edith Hamilton, *Mythology*. New York: New American Library, 1940. Hamilton's excellent retelling of the Greek myths is still considered by many to be the best and most entertaining overview of its kind.

Rhoda A. Hendricks, trans., *Classical Gods and Heroes: Myths as Told by the Ancient Authors*. New York: Morrow Quill, 1974. A collection of easy-to-read translations of famous Greek myths and tales, as told by ancient Greek and Roman writers, including Homer, Hesiod, Pindar, Apollodorus, Ovid, and Virgil.

Homer, *Odyssey*. Trans. E. V. Rieu. Baltimore: Penguin Books, 1961. This is one of the better translations of Homer's great epic about the exciting adventures of one of the heroes of the Trojan War.

Livy, *The History of Rome from Its Foundation*. Books 1–5 published as *Livy: The Early History of Rome*. Trans. Aubrey de Sélincourt. New York: Penguin Books, 1971. An excellent translation of these parts of Livy's massive and masterful history, written during Rome's golden literary age of the late first century B.C.; contains the most extensive available primary-source descriptions of Romulus and the Roman foundation.

Stewart Perowne, *Roman Mythology*. London: Paul Hamlyn, 1969. This volume by Perowne, the noted historian, archaeologist, and author of several important works about Rome, is well written and nicely illustrated.

Virgil, *Aeneid*. Trans. Patric Dickinson. New York: New American Library, 1961. An excellent translation of the epic poem that constitutes the single major source for the legends of the Roman founder Aeneas.

Philip Wilkinson, *The Illustrated Dictionary of Mythology*. New York: Dorling Kindersley, 1998. This well-written, handsomely mounted book contains short overviews of hundreds of mythological characters, facts, and stories of peoples from around the world.

Additional Works Consulted

Hartley B. Alexander, *The Mythology of All Races. Volume 10: North American.* New York: Cooper Square, 1964.

Apollonius of Rhodes, *Argonautica*, published as *The Voyage of the Argo*. Trans. E. V. Rieu. New York: Penguin Books, 1971.

Richard Barber, ed., *The Arthurian Legends: An Illustrated Anthology*. New York: Peter Bedrick Books, 1979.

R. H. Barrow, *The Romans*. Baltimore: Penguin Books, 1964.

Henry A. Bellows, trans., *Poetic Edda*. New York: Biblo and Tannen, 1969.

C. M. Bowra, *The Greek Experience*. New York: New American Library, 1957.

Abbie F. Brown, *In the Days of the Giants*. Boston: Houghton Mifflin, 1906.

Joseph Campbell, *Myths to Live By*. New York: Bantam Books, 1972.

Lionel Casson, *The Ancient Mariners: Seafarers and Sea Fighters of the Mediterranean in Ancient Times*. New York: Macmillan, 1959.

Nora K. Chadwick and Barry Cunliffe, *The Celts*. New York: Penguin Books, 1998.

T. J. Cornell, *The Beginnings of Rome: Italy and Rome from the Bronze Age to the Punic Wars (c. 1000–264 B.C.)*. London: Routledge, 1995.

Stephanie Dalley, trans., *Myths from Mesopotamia*. New York: Oxford University Press, 1989.

Jacqueline de Romilly, *A Short History of Greek Literature*. Chicago: University of Chicago Press, 1985.

Mircea Eliade, ed., *Essential Sacred Writings from Around the World*. San Francisco: HarperCollins, 1967.

Peter B. Ellis, *The Celtic Empire: The First Millennium of Celtic History, c. 1000 B.C.–51 A.D.* Durham, NC: Carolina Academic Press, 1990.

Charles Freeman, *The Greek Achievement: The Foundation of the Western World*. New York: Viking/Penguin, 1999.

Jane F. Gardner, *Roman Myths*. Austin: University of Texas Press, 1993.

Sam D. Gill and Irene F. Sullivan, *Dictionary of Native American Mythology*. New York: Oxford University Press, 1992.

Norma L. Goodrich, *Ancient Myths*. New York: New American Library, 1960.

Miranda J. Green, *Celtic Myths*. Austin: University of Texas Press, 1993.

Frederick E. Hoxie, ed., *Encyclopedia of North American Indians*. New York: Houghton Mifflin, 1996.

Samuel N. Kramer, *Cradle of Civilization*. New York: Time-Life, 1967.

———, ed., *Mythologies of the Ancient World*. Garden City, NY: Doubleday, 1961.

J. V. Luce, *Lost Atlantis*, New York: McGraw Hill, 1969.

P. M. Matarasso, trans., *The Quest of the Holy Grail*. New York: Penguin Books, 1969.

Mark P. O. Morford and Robert J. Lenardon, *Classical Mythology*. New York: Longman, 1985.

John Pinsent, *Greek Mythology*. New York: Peter Bedrick Books, 1986.

James B. Pritchard, ed., *Ancient Near Eastern Texts Relating to the Old Testament*. Princeton, NJ: Princeton University Press, 1969.

W. H. D. Rouse, *Gods, Heroes, and Men of Ancient Greece*. New York: New American Library, 1957.

Sallust, *Conspiracy of Catiline*, in *Sallust: The Jugurthine War/The Conspiracy of Catiline*. Trans. S. A. Handford. New York: Penguin Books, 1988.

Snorri Sturluson, *The Prose Edda: Tales from Norse Mythology*. Trans. Jean I. Young. Berkeley: University of California Press, 1966.

Carl Waldman, *Atlas of the North American Indian*. New York: Facts On File, 1985.

Index

Picture Credits

Cover Photo: © Charles and Josette Lenars/Corbis
Archive Photos, 46
© Bettmann/Corbis, 19, 28
Brown Brothers, 35, 47, 79
© Burstein Collection/Corbis, 62, 65, 69
© Richard A. Cooke/Corbis, 95
© Corbis, 38
Fortean Picture Library, 13, 81
FPG International, 91
© Historical Picture Archives/Corbis, 33
Hulton Getty Collection/Archive Photos, 8, 45, 55, 61, 64, 82
Erich Lessing/Art Resource, NY, 48, 54
Library of Congress, 39, 40, 41, 94
© David Muench/Corbis, 90
North Wind Picture Archives, 30, 36, 51, 59, 71, 74, 75, 89
© Gianni Dagli Orti/Corbis, 15
Photofest, 9
Scala/Art Resource, NY, 17
Stock Montage, 22, 77, 84
Tate Gallery, London/Art Resource, NY, 68

About the Author

Historian Don Nardo has written several volumes about ancient cultures and their religious beliefs and mythologies, among them *Life in Ancient Athens*, *The Persian Empire*, *Greek and Roman Mythology*, and *Egyptian Mythology*. Mr. Nardo is also the editor of *The Greenhaven Encyclopedia of Greek and Roman Mythology*. He lives with his wife Christine in Massachusetts.